Electric Guitar Primer Deluxe Edition

by
Bert Casey

Video & Audio Downloads Available
download@cvls.com

INTRODUCTION

The *Electric Guitar Primer Deluxe Edition* with DVD & audio CD will quickly transform you from an absolute beginner into a student/guitarist with a full understanding of the fundamentals and techniques of guitar playing. This clear, step-by-step method includes many photographs, large easy-to-read notation and tablature, and a sequence of learning that has been meticulously developed and tested over a 20 year period. With each new song, you will learn new techniques to establish a firm foundation that will enable you to enjoy playing guitar for many years. No wonder the *Electric Guitar Primer Deluxe Edition* is the first choice of over 2,000 stores throughout the United States and Canada.

THE AUTHOR

Bert Casey, the author of this book, has been a professional performer and teacher in the Atlanta area for over 30 years. He plays several instruments (acoustic guitar, electric guitar, bass guitar, mandolin, banjo, ukulele, and flute) and has written seven other courses (*Acoustic Guitar Primer*, *Acoustic Guitar Book 2*, *Bass Guitar Primer*, *Ukulele Primer, Mandolin Primer*, *Flatpicking Guitar Songs*, and *Bluegrass Fakebook*). Bert performed several years in Atlanta and the Southeast with his bands Home Remedy and Blue Moon. His talent and willingness to share have helped thousands of students learn and experience the joy of playing a musical instrument.

WATCH & LEARN PRODUCTS REALLY WORK

30 years ago, Watch & Learn revolutionized music instructional courses by developing thorough, step-by-step instructional methods combined with clear, easy-to-understand graphics that were tested for effectiveness on beginners before publication. This concept, which has dramatically improved the understanding and success of beginning students, has evolved into the Watch & Learn mastermind of authors, editors, teachers, and artists that continue to set the standard of music instruction today. This has resulted in sales of almost 2 million products since 1979. This high quality course will significantly increase your success and enjoyment while playing the guitar.

CD, DVD, & VIDEO COUNTER

The CD, DVD, and video counters are included in this book to show where each lesson is located on the companion CD, DVD, or video. Use your remote control on the DVD or CD player to skip to the track you want. Check the counter number as it appears on screen in the video and then scan to the exact location on the video.

Followup Courses

There are two excellent followup courses to the *Electric Guitar Primer*:

Blues Guitar Deluxe Edition by Peter Vogl is a followup to the Electric Guitar course and teaches more advanced rhythm to the 12 Bar Blues and soloing using the minor pentatonic and blues scales. It covers many popular techniques that blues players use and also contains a hot licks section.
    Book/DVD/CD $15.95

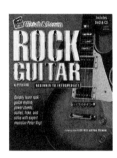

Introduction to Rock Guitar by Peter Vogl is another followup course that teaches more advanced rhythm techniques and lead playing using the minor pentatonic scales. It shows all the techniques that legendary rock guitarists use to get those famous sounds. It also contains a hot licks section.
    Book/DVD/CD $15.95

These products are available at your local store, on our website - **cvls.com**, or send a check including $5.00 shipping and handling to the following address:

Watch & Learn, Inc.
1882 Queens Way
Atlanta, GA 30341
800-416-7088

TABLE OF CONTENTS

SECTION IV - Scales

APPENDIX

AUDIO CD

The accompanying CD contains all of the lessons in the book up through Section III. Each lesson is recorded in its entirety. The songs are played twice, a slow version with guitar and an up tempo version using a full band (guitar, bass, drums, keyboards, and vocals). The following list shows the track number for the up tempo version of each of the songs on the CD. The CD is mixed in stereo with the guitar on the left channel and the other instruments on the right channel so that you can adjust the guitar volume to suit your taste. The CD contains the following songs, which are recorded by permission:

SECTION I
GETTING STARTED

PARTS OF THE GUITAR

 2:50

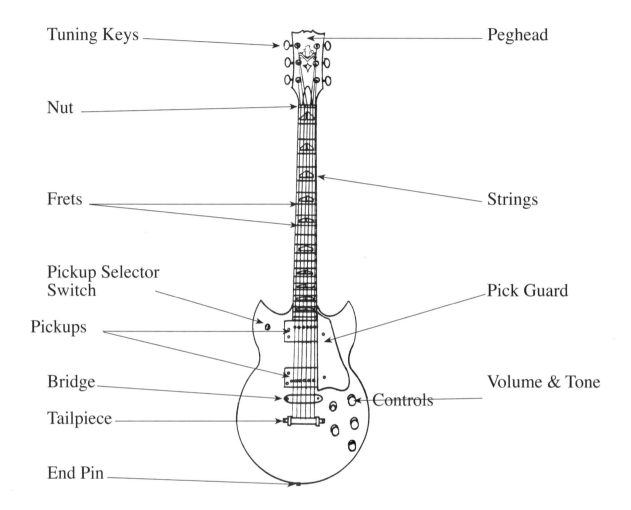

Tuning Keys

Nut

Frets

Pickup Selector
Switch

Pickups

Bridge

Tailpiece

End Pin

Peghead

Strings

Pick Guard

Volume & Tone

Controls

You will need a guitar amplifier and a good cord that does not buzz or crackle. We recommend a new cord with a 5 year warranty. The amplifier should be in good condition and not produce noise or hum. There are many combinations of wattage and speaker size in guitar amps. Get the best sounding amp that you can afford. A nice feature is a headphone jack so that you can practice without disturbing anyone.

You should also be able to get your choice of a clear sound or a distorted sound (overdrive) from the amplifier. As you progress, you may want to add some effects pedals to get a wider variety of guitar sounds, but for now we will use the amplifier by itself.

Get to know the folks at your local music store. They can be a great help with supplies, lessons, & advice.

HOLDING THE GUITAR

 3:05

Many guitarists are self taught and have developed their own unique and sometimes unorthodox styles of holding and playing the guitar. In this book we will be using the most common techniques that are approved and taught by instructors.

At first you will be holding the guitar sitting down. Use a straight back chair so that you can sit with good posture and have free arm movement without banging the guitar or your arms on the furniture.

Sit erect with both feet on the floor and the guitar resting on your right thigh. The guitar should be braced against your chest with the right forearm so that the neck of the guitar doesn't move when you change hand positions.

In the standing position, use a strap and brace the guitar against your body in the same way as you would sitting down.

 TIP *Always use a case or gig bag when transporting your instrument from one place to another.*

TUNING THE GUITAR

Before playing the guitar, it must be tuned to standard pitch. We will discuss several ways to tune the guitar. If you have a piano at home, it can be used as a tuning source. The following diagram shows which note on the piano to tune each open string of the guitar to.

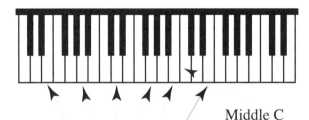

Middle C

Note - If your piano hasn't been tuned recently, the guitar may not agree perfectly with a pitch pipe or tuning fork. Some older pianos are tuned a half step below standard pitch. In this case, use one of the following methods to tune.

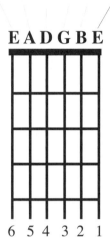

E A D G B E

6 5 4 3 2 1

ELECTRONIC TUNER

An electronic tuner is the fastest and most accurate way to tune a guitar. I highly recommend getting one. They are available for under $30.

PITCH PIPE

Pitch pipes are an easy and portable way of tuning a guitar. They may be obtained at a local music store with complete instructions.

DVD OR CD

It is recommended that you tune your guitar to the DVD or CD that accompanies this book so that you will be in tune when you play along with the songs and exercises.

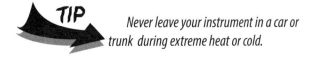

Never leave your instrument in a car or trunk during extreme heat or cold.

RELATIVE TUNING

Relative tuning means to tune the guitar to itself and is used in the following situations:

1. When you do not have an electronic tuner or other source to tune from.
2. When you have only one note to tune from.

In the following example we will tune all of the strings to the 6th string of the guitar, which is an E note.

1. Place the ring finger of the left hand behind the fifth fret of the 6th string to fret the 1st note. Tune the 5th string open (not fretted) until it sounds like the 6th string fretted at the 5th fret.
2. Fret the 5th string at the 5th fret. Tune the 4th string open (not fretted) until it sounds like the 5th string at the 5th fret.
3. Fret the 4th string at the 5th fret. Tune the 3rd string open until it sounds like the 4th string at the 5th fret.
4. Fret the 3rd string at the 4th fret. Tune the 2nd string until it sounds like the 3rd string at the 4th fret.
5. Fret the 2nd string at the 5th fret. Tune the 1st string open until it sounds like the 2nd string at the 5th fret.

Now repeat the above procedure to fine tune the guitar. Until your ear develops, have your teacher or a guitar playing friend check the tuning to make sure it is correct.

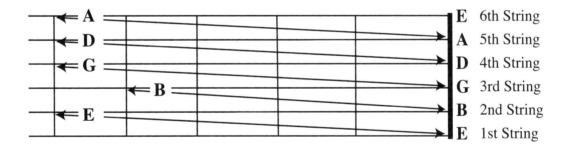

The following diagram of the guitar fret board illustrates the above procedure.

Note - Old dull strings lose their tonal qualities and sometimes tune incorrectly. Check with your teacher or favorite music store to make sure your strings are in good playing condition.

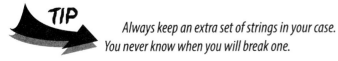

Always keep an extra set of strings in your case.
You never know when you will break one.

4

USING THE PICK

Selecting The Pick

When you visit a music store, you will notice that there are almost as many pick styles and shapes as there are guitar players. A pick should feel comfortable in your hand and produce a clear, clean tone when picking or strumming the strings. This is the most popular shaped pick.

Holding The Pick

The grip on a pick should provide control while feeling comfortable. The most common way of holding the pick is to curl the right index finger (Figure 1), place the pick in the first joint of the index finger with the point facing straight out (Figure 2) , and then place the thumb firmly on the pick with the thumb parallel to the first joint (Figure 3). Listen to the DVD for further clarification.

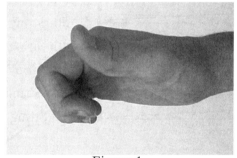

Figure 1

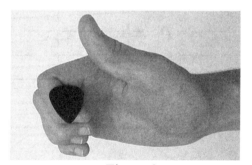

Figure 2

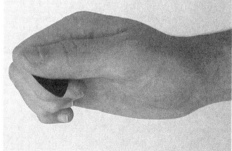

Figure 3

 *Keep many extra picks around. They like to disappear, much like socks.*

RIGHT HAND POSITION

   Position the right hand so that the pick strikes the strings between the bridge and the fretboard. The right forearm should be braced against the body of the guitar so that the right hand falls into a position towards the center of the body of the guitar. Do not play directly over the pickups because the pick could accidently strike them and cause unwanted noise.

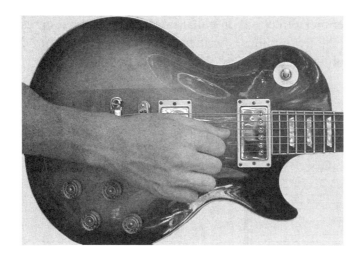

The right hand should be free with no part of the hand or wrist touching the guitar.

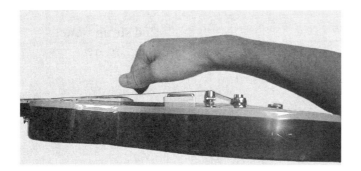

EXERCISE 1

   Practice strumming down on all the guitar strings (towards the floor) while making sure that you hold the pick correctly. Check your hand position to make sure that it is also correct. Start your strum at the 6th string and end it just below the 1st string.

 **TIP**   *Use a guitar cloth to clean your guitar and wipe it down after you play.*

TABLATURE

This book is written in both tablature and standard music notation. If you wish to learn to read music, consult your local music store for a good book or ask you music teacher for an explanation. We will explain tablature because it is easy to learn if you are teaching yourself and because a lot of popular guitar music is available in tablature.

Tablature is a system for writing music that shows the proper string and fret to play and which fingers to use. It also shows the proper pick direction. In guitar tablature, each line represents a string on the guitar. If the string is to be fretted, the fret number is written on the appropriate line. Otherwise a "0" is written. Study the examples below until you understand them thoroughly.

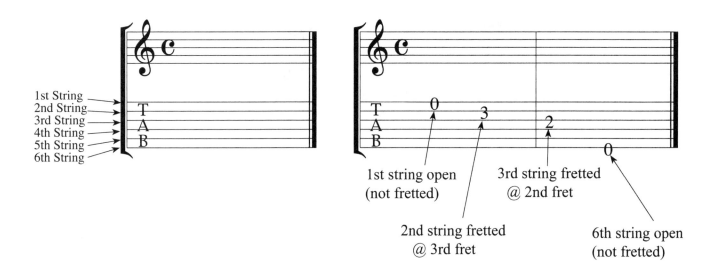

The music will be divided into two sets of lines (staffs) with guitar notation on the top line and tablature on the bottom line.

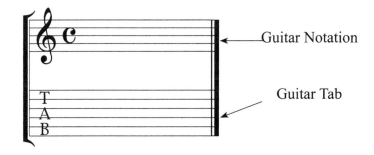

Learning music theory will help you understand how music is written.

7

OUR FIRST NOTES

 9:05 7-10

PLAYING NOTES ON THE 6TH STRING

We will now play the notes on the 6th string of the guitar starting in the Key of C . It will be helpful to listen to the CD or DVD as you study this page.

E NOTE

Pluck the 6th string open with a down stroke (towards the floor) with your pick to produce an E note. The 6th string is the fattest string, which is the closest to you when holding the guitar properly. The E note is written in both music and tablature to the right. Play the E note several times while listening to the CD or DVD.

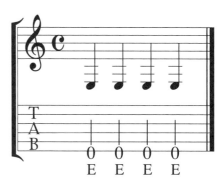

F NOTE

Place the tip of the left index finger directly behind the first fret of the 6th string (note pictures below). Pick the 6th string with a down stroke to produce an F note.

Front View	Top View	Side View

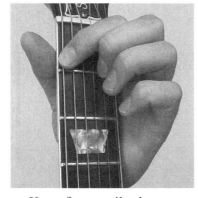 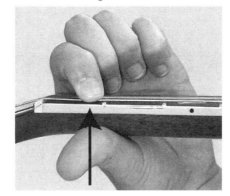 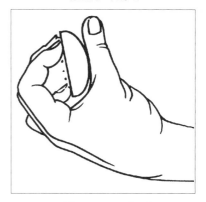

Keep fingernails short   Use fingertips   Fingers arched

Note -The left thumb should be placed directly under the 1st fret of the guitar using the elevated thumb placement as shown above and on page 60.

The F note is written in both tablature and standard notation to the right. Practice the F note along with the CD or DVD until you can play it clearly.

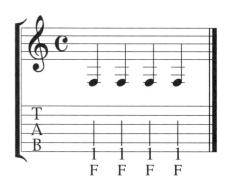

 *Don't store your guitar in the attic or basement. Extreme dryness or dampness can be bad.*

8

G NOTE

Place the tip of your left ring finger directly behind the 3rd fret of the 6th string. Pick down to produce a G note.

The G note is written in both tablature and standard music notation below. Practice the G note along with the CD until you can play it clearly.

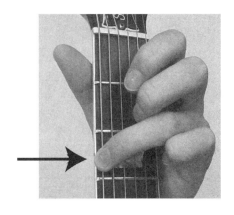

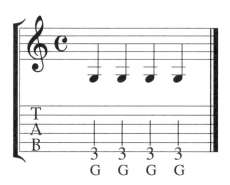

EXERCISE 2

We'll now combine the E, F, & G notes into one exercise. Practice these notes until you can play them smoothly and clearly. Make sure you use all downstrokes with the right hand.

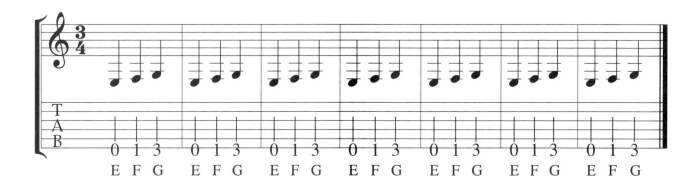

Note - We are using the same left hand finger as the fret we are playing (1st finger at 1st fret, 2nd finger at 2nd fret, 3rd finger at 3rd fret). This is referred to as "frets and fingers the same".

Practicing a little each day is better than practicing a lot all at once.

NOTES ON THE 5TH STRING

With your left thumb still positioned under the 2nd fret, we will play notes on the 5th string.

A NOTE

Pick the fifth string open (not fretted) with a down stroke to produce an A note as shown to the right.

B NOTE

Place the tip of your left middle finger directly behind the 2nd fret of the 5th string. Pick down on the 5th string to produce a B note as shown to the right.

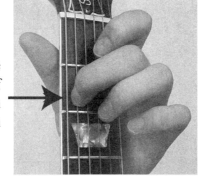

C NOTE

Place the tip of your left ring finger directly behind the 3rd fret on the 5th string. Pick down on the 5th string to produce a C note as shown to the right.

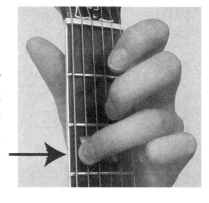

EXERCISE 3

We'll now play the A, B, & C notes together. Again, practice this exercise until you can play all three notes smoothly and clearly.

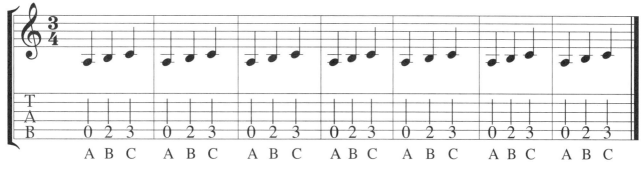

 TIP

Practice new songs slowly and relaxed. Work on speed after you can play it perfectly.

NOTES ON THE 4TH STRING

 11:30

13

The notes on the 4th string are played on the same frets as the notes on the 5th string, just one string higher. Use the same left hand fingering (frets & fingers the same) and pick with a downstroke.

EXERCISE 4

Listen to the CD or DVD to play Exercise 4.

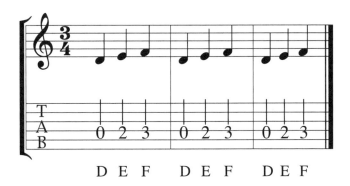

PLAYING NOTES ON THE 3RD, 2ND & 1ST STRINGS

EXERCISE 5 - 3rd String

Play the notes on the 3rd string as shown to the right. Notice that we are only playing 2 notes, G & A, on the 3rd string.

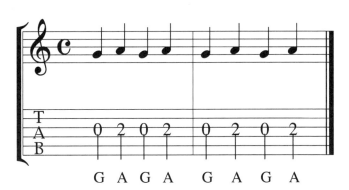

EXERCISE 6 - 2nd String

Here are the notes on the 2nd string - B, C, & D.

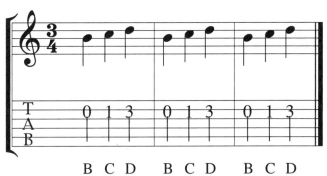

EXERCISE 7 - 1st String

And finally, the E, F, & G notes on the 1st string.

Working with a metronome helps you practice slowly and gradually increase speed.

USING ALL THE STRINGS

It is faster to learn the strings in pairs rather than all 6 strings at once. Practice the 6th & 5th strings together, the 4th & 3rd strings together, and the 2nd & 1st strings together. After you have gotten smooth playing each pair of strings, then play all 6 strings in order as follows:

EXERCISE 8

Practice the notes on the 6th & 5th strings as shown below until you have memorized them.

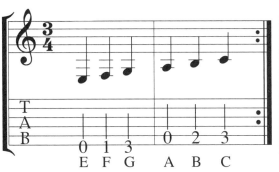

WALKING THE BASS

Practice this melody until you are comfortable playing it.

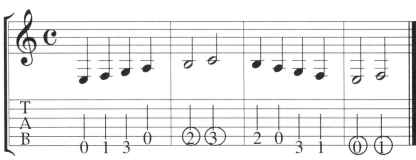

EXERCISE 9

Play the notes on the 4th & 3rd strings as shown until you have memorized them.

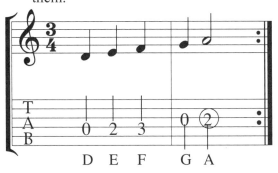

TOOLING AROUND

Play this melody on the 4th & 3rd strings.

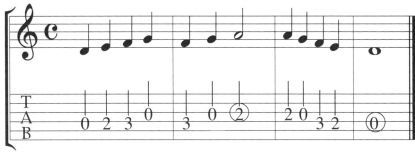

EXERCISE 10

Now play the notes on the 2nd & 1st strings until you have them memorized.

PLAYING ON HIGH

Here's a melody to play on the first two strings.

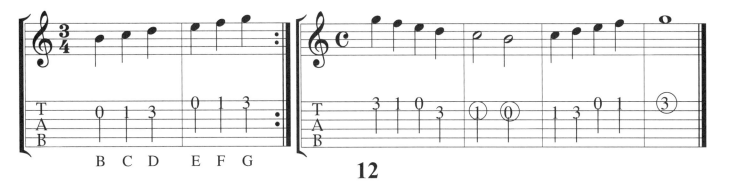

12

EXERCISE 11

Now we'll combine the notes we've learned so far to play all of the notes in a C scale in the first or open position.

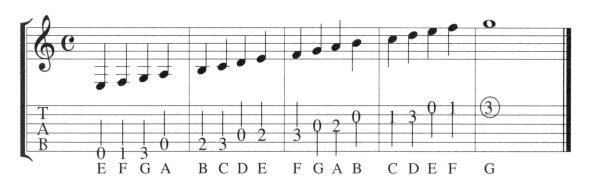

EXERCISE 12

Now play the reverse of the previous exercise by starting with the highest note and working your way back down the scale.

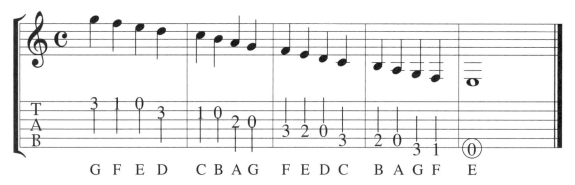

Note - You should memorize this scale so that you can concentrate on your hand positions.

We will now use the C scale to play some more simple melodies so you can practice moving your fingers around.

ETUDE IN C

Here's a melody on the first three strings.

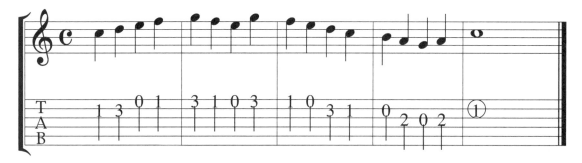

BASS ETUDE

Now play this melody using the bottom three strings.

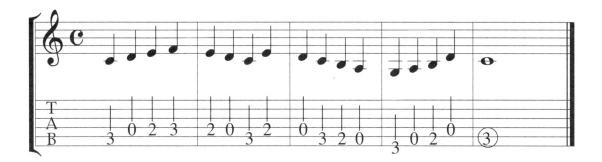

TIMING

As we go through the book, we will explain about timing and note values. The following symbols show the note values for tablature and music notation.

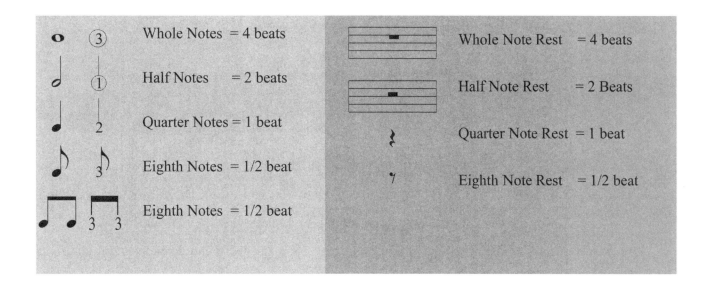

Note - From this point on, the DVD follows a different sequence than the book. Check the lesson plan on the next page as well as the Table of Contents for the corresponding positions on the CD or DVD.

TIP

If your practice sounds good all the time, you're not challenging yourself.

Author's Note

This book was written to take the student step by step through learning to play the guitar as if he were taking private lessons. With that in mind, you should work on Sections II, III, & IV of this book simultaneously. Instead of going through this book page by page in sequence, you should take one lesson from each section to work on each practice session. Typically, beginning students would make faster progress in Section IV than in Section III, and Section II would be the hardest of all. Each section is very important and should be mastered.

I've included a suggested lesson plan to give you an idea of how I would present this material in private lessons. Each student will learn at different rates, so you will learn to modify this to suit your individual learning speeds.

Lesson Plan

Week	Section I	Section II	Section III	Section IV		
1	pages 1-11	pages 17-19		p. 33-34	Ex. 26-28	
2	page 12	p. 20	Song 1	p. 34	Song 11	
3	page 13	p. 20	Song 2	p. 35	Song 12	
4	page 14	p. 21	Ex. 18	p. 36	Song 13	
5		p. 22	Song 3	p. 37-38	Ex. 30-33	p. 55 Ex. 51
6		p. 23	Song 4	p. 38	Song 14	p. 55 Ex. 52
7		p. 24	Song 5	p. 39	Song 15	p. 56 Pattern I
8		p. 25	Song 6	p. 40	Song 16	p. 56 Pattern II
9		p. 26-27	Song 7	p. 41	Song 17	p. 57 Pattern III
10		p. 28	Song 8	p. 42	Song 18	p. 57 Pattern IV
11		p. 29-30	Song 9	p. 43-45	Song 19	p. 58 Pattern V
12		p. 31	Song 10	p. 46	Song 20	p. 59 Minor Scales

The next parts of this book concentrate on rhythm techniques. There are three basic ways to play rhythm on the guitar:

> **1. Strumming Chords or Fingerpicking Chords** - We will learn chords and several common strums in Section II.
> **2. Riffs** - Riffs are partial chords where you are only playing 2 or 3 strings at a time instead of all 6 strings. We'll concentrate on this technique in Section III.
> **3. Melody Lines** - This is derived from playing scales where you are only playing one string at a time. We'll cover this more in Section IV.

All three approaches are commonly used and are often combined and alternated in the same song. If you have more than one guitar part being played in a song, they will commonly use different rhythm techniques. We will study these techniques one by one in the next three sections.

 *Try to find friends who play. Playing with others is great fun & you learn new things as well.*

SECTION II
CHORDS & STRUMMING
(PLAYING POPULAR SONGS)

OUR FIRST CHORDS

The basis of all good guitar playing is chords. We will now start noting chords with the left hand and strumming with the right hand to play rhythm. We will start in the key of A because that is a common key for rock playing and because the chords are fairly easy. The first three chords we will play are A, D, and E.

THE A CHORD

An A chord consists of the 1st, 3rd, & 5th notes of the A scale (A, C#, E). Now play an A chord as shown in the following diagrams:

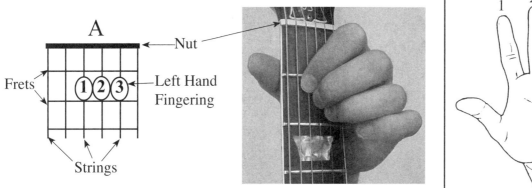

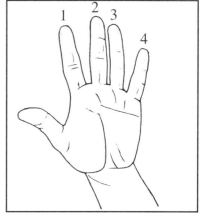

Check the following to make sure you are using good technique:

1. The bottom joint of the thumb should be placed on the center of the guitar neck. See pictures on page 60 for elevated thumb placement.

2. The fingers should be arched so that the tips of the fingers fret the strings. Do not touch an adjacent string with one of your fingers. Check the diagrams on page 8 for correct placement.

EXERCISE 13

Form the A chord and strum the guitar from the 6th string down (towards the floor) in one smooth stroke.

A - A - A - A - A - A - A - A - A - A - A

Note - Some people have trouble with the A chord because of the size of their fingers. If you have problems after practicing for several days, try the alternate fingerings for A as shown on page 60.

Note - Some method books use beginner chords where only 3 or 4 strings are played. We, however, use full 6 string chords because that is what is commonly played on the guitar. A beginner usually takes 6 to 8 weeks to become fully comfortable with these chords. Keep practicing and your hand and finger muscles will strengthen and stretch so that the chords will become easier. Check the lesson plan on page 15 to make sure you are learning all the techniques in the correct order.

THE D CHORD

A D chord consists of the 1st, 3rd, & 5th notes of the D scale (D, F#, A). We'll now play a D chord as shown below:

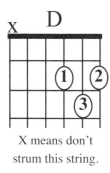

X means don't
strum this string.

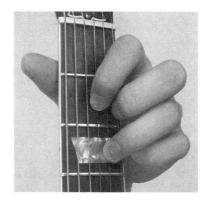

EXERCISE 14

Strum the D Chord from the 5th string down, towards the floor, in one smooth stroke.

D - D - D - D - D - D - D - D

EXERCISE 15

Practice changing between the two chords you have learned so far. Strum once on the A chord, change to the D chord and strum once, go back to the A chord , etc.

A - D - A - D - A - D - A - D - A - D - A - D - A - D - A - D - A - D - A - D

BUZZING, MUFFLED, & UNCLEAR NOTES

If you aren't getting a clear distinct sound when playing, check the following problem areas:

1. Not pressing hard enough with the left hand. Press the strings firmly but not so hard as to be painful.
2. Fingers too far from the fret wires or on top of the frets. The fingers of the left hand should be directly behind the frets. Check the diagrams on pages 8 & 17.
3. Fingers touching an adjacent string. Make sure your fingers are arched properly.
4. Fingernails too long. Trim your fingernails so that the tips of the fingers can press down on the strings.

 Purchase a music stand. People who use one tend to practice up to 30% longer.

THE E CHORD

We'll now add a third chord to our repertoire, the E chord, which is composed of the 1st, 3rd, & 5th notes of the E scale (E, G#, B).

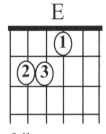
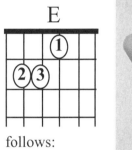

EXERCISE 16

Form the E chord and strum down towards the floor as follows:

E - E - E - E - E - E - E - E - E

EXERCISE 17

Now practice changing between all three chords as follows:

A - E - A - E - A - E - A - E - A - E - A - E - A - E - A - E - A - E - A - E - A - E

A - D - E - A - D - E - A - D - E - A - D - E - A - D - E - A - D - E - A - D - E

Note - Make sure that your fingers are properly arched and that they move perpendicular to the strings. Do not bend the strings as this will cause the chords to sound out of tune.

HAND EYE COORDINATION

It will take a while to get the hang of changing between these chords. After you get comfortable with them you'll want to eliminate one of the steps you've been taking, looking at your hands. First practice the chord changes, strum down once on each chord, and don't look at your right hand.

After you've tried this for a while, practice the changes without looking at either hand. Just close your eyes and go through the same exercises.

At first you had three steps before you could strum a chord: looking at the book, looking at your left hand, and looking at your right hand. To build your speed and proficiency you'll have to eliminate these steps by practicing without looking at your hands or the book.

Keep your guitar looking good with guitar polish. Never use furniture polish or cleaner.

THE FIRST SONGS

SONG 1

Listen to Song 1 on the accompanying CD, **Louie, Louie**, to practice the following technique. This was made popular by the **Kingsmen** in the 60's.

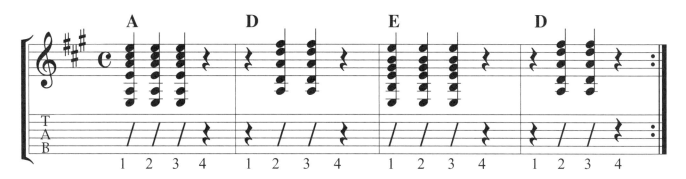

Note - / = strum down towards the floor. ♩ = 1/4 note rest. Count 1 2 3 4 very evenly. Strum down on 1, 2, & 3, and rest (do not play) on 4. In the second measure, form a D chord, rest on 1, strum down on 2 & 3, and rest on 4. The 3rd measure uses the same right hand technique as the first measure, but you are playing an E chord. The 4th measure is the same as the 2nd. Listen to the CD to get the proper timing.

SONG 2

Listen to Song 2 on the CD, **Wild Thing**, to play this technique. This was a hit for **Jimi Hendrix** and for **The Trogs**.

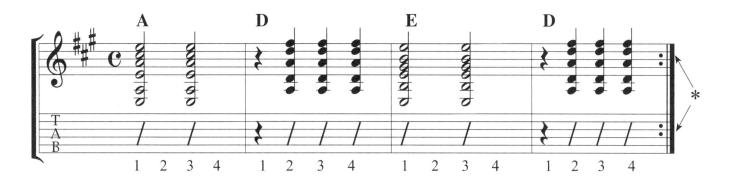

Note - In the first measure, strum on 1, rest on 2, strum on 3, and rest on 4. In the second measure, rest on 1, strum on 2, 3, & 4. The 3rd measure is the same as the 1st except that you are playing an E chord. Again listen to the CD for the proper timing.

* The repeat signs mean to play the measures between them again. Keep repeating these measures until you feel comfortable and are producing clear, distinct notes.

DOWN UP STRUM

A very common rhythm technique uses an up stroke along with the down stroke. The down stroke is the same strum that we've been using. Starting with the 6th string, strum down towards the floor in one smooth motion, stopping just below the 1st string. To play an upstroke, strum up (towards the ceiling). This strum is much shorter than the down stroke because you stop at the 4th string. You play all six strings on the down stroke and play the first four strings on the up stroke. The following diagrams illustrate this.

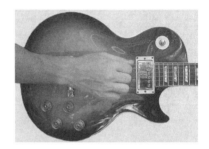
Start of down stoke

End of down stroke

End of up stroke

EXERCISE 18

Using up strokes means we will be playing eighth notes. We're still using 4 beats per measure, but we'll be dividing them up. Count out loud very evenly 1 2 & 3 & 4 . You will strum down on the numbers and strum up on the &'s. This strum would be down, down-up, down-up, down. The up stroke is shown as /\. Play along to the CD or DVD to get the proper feel.

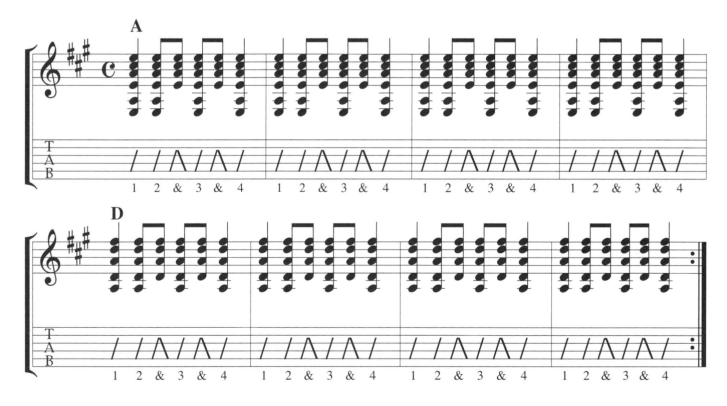

SONG 3

Now we'll combine this strum with the A, D, & E chords to play a very common chord progression. Play along with Song 3, **Old Time Rock & Roll**, on the CD or DVD to get the proper timing.

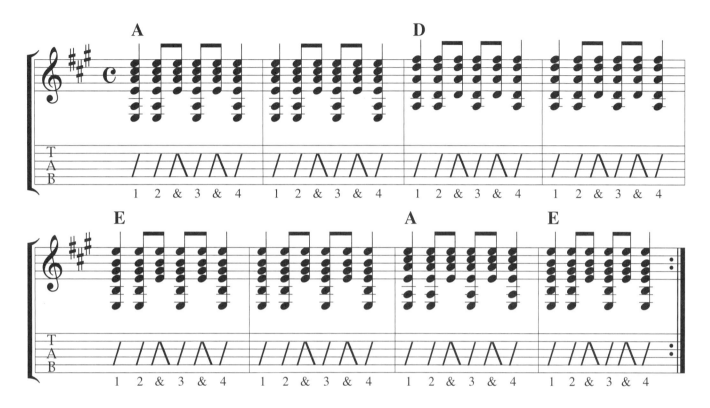

Make sure you play this very slowly at first. Practice changing the chords smoothly and strum to the proper rhythm by playing along with the CD or DVD. There should be no pause in the music for the chord changes. Take your time and get comfortable coordinating the left and right hands. You should also memorize this song and play without looking at either hand or at the book. Try to visualize what each hand is doing so that you get a clear mental picture of your hand movements. When you are able to do all of this smoothly, then speed the song up gradually, until you can play along with the faster versions on the CD. Make sure to use repeat play on your CD player and play along many times.

The next few songs that we'll use are generic chord progressions that would fit many different tunes. You'll probably recognize several examples as we play them.

Keep your instrument from being knocked over. Purchase a guitar stand.

We will now play a 12 Bar Blues progression using the same strum and chords. We will also play this song in Section III using rock & roll riffs. This corresponds to **12 Bar Blues** on the DVD.

SONG 4
JOHNNY B. GOODE

Written by
Chuck Berry

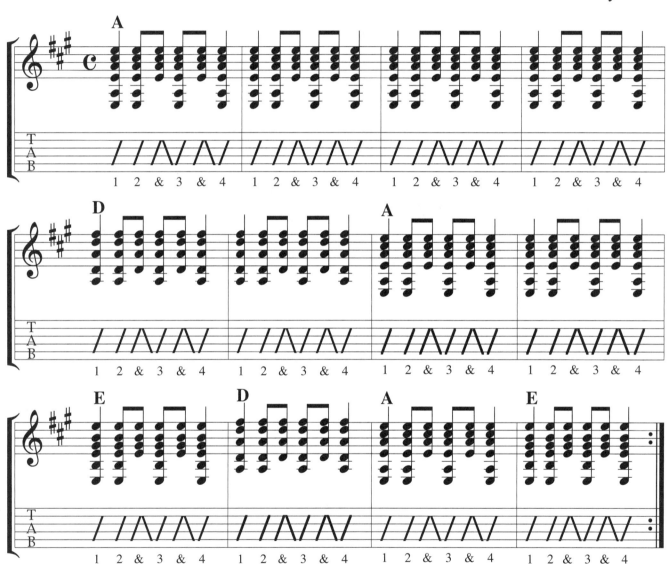

Strings should be replaced at least every three months, sometimes sooner.

MINOR CHORDS

EXERCISE 19

We'll now add some new chords to our repertoire and use them with the strum we just learned. A minor chord is the 1st, b3rd, & 5th notes of that scale. Play the E minor (Em) chord (E, G, B).

EXERCISE 20

Play the A minor chord (A, C, E) as shown below and then practice changing between the two chords.

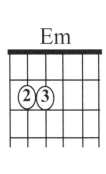

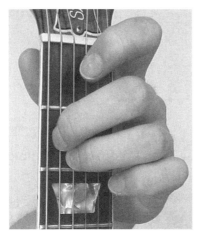

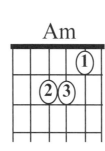

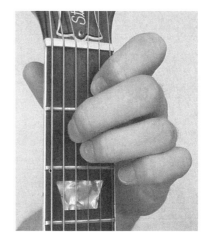

Em - Am - Em - Am - Em - Am - Em - Am - Em - Am - Em - Am

SONG 5

We'll now combine these two chords into a song in the key of Em. Listen to Song 5 on the CD, **Miss You**, or **Minor Melody** on the DVD to play the following song that was a hit for **The Rolling Stones**.

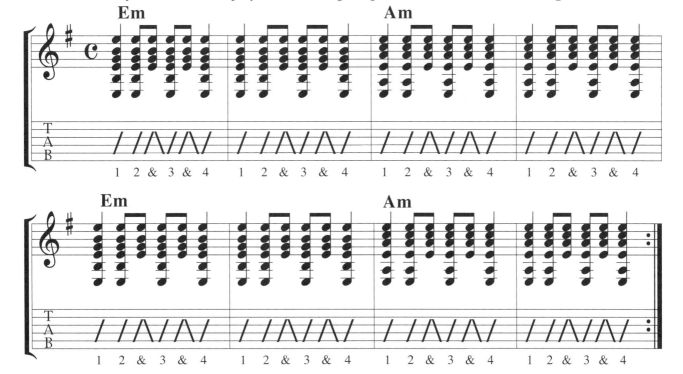

B7 CHORD

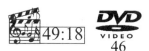

A seventh chord is the 1st, 3rd, 5th, & b7th notes of that scale. We'll add a B7 chord (B, D#, F#, A) to the ones we already know in order to play another popular song. Practice changing between the Em & B7 chords.

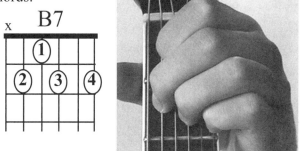

Em - B7 - Em - B7 - Em - B7

SONG 6

Listen to Song 6 on the CD, **Black Magic Woman**, or **Latin Rock** on the DVD to play along. Use the same right hand strum we've been practicing. This song was made popular by **Santana**.

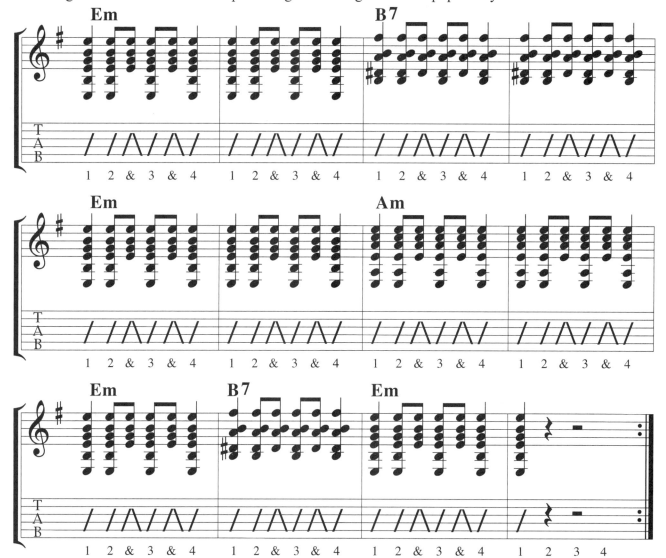

MORE MAJOR CHORDS

G CHORD

We'll be adding new chords on every page but don't get discouraged if you have trouble with them. Just keep practicing and you'll get the hang of them. It just takes time.

EXERCISE 21

Practice the G chord (G, B, D) and the chord changes shown below:

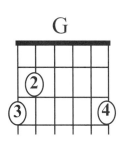

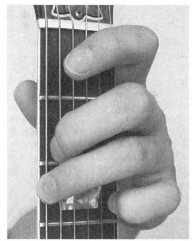

D - G - A - D - G - A - D - G - A - D - G - A - D - G - A - D - G - A

EXERCISE 22

Here's a variation of the basic strum. This strum would be down, down up, up down up, on the beats 1, 2&, &4&.

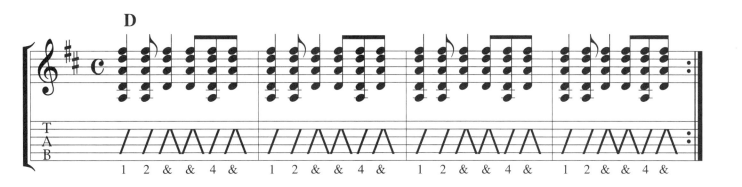

This strum will have a slightly syncopated or swing feel to it. Listen and practice with the CD or DVD until you get the proper feel.

SONG 7

The following song is in the Key of D. Listen to Song 7 on the CD, **Don't Be Cruel**, or **Rockabilly** on the DVD to play along. This was made popular by **Elvis Presley** and **Cheap Trick**.

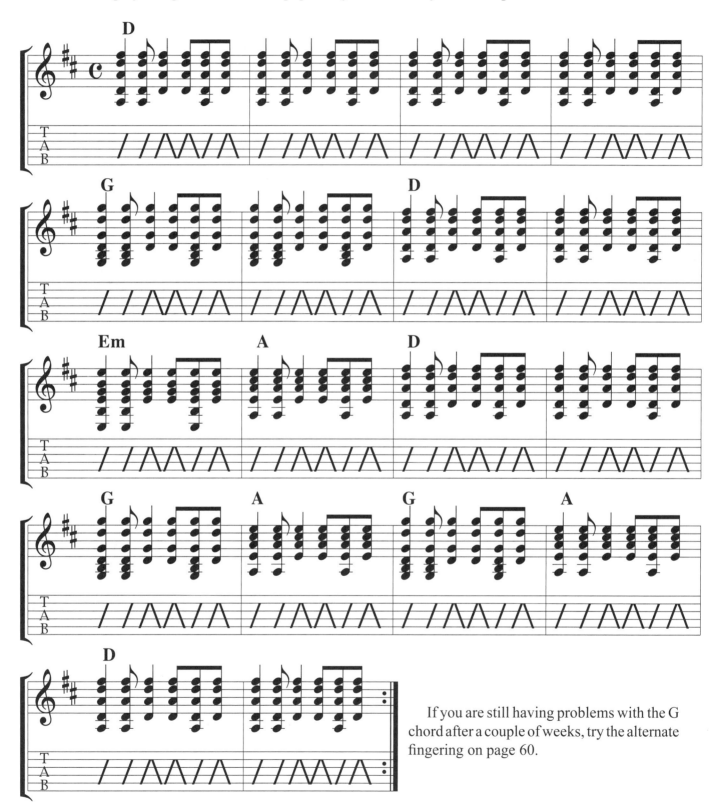

If you are still having problems with the G chord after a couple of weeks, try the alternate fingering on page 60.

C CHORD

The C chord (C, E, G) is another common chord. Practice the chord changes shown below. Move your 2nd & 3rd fingers as a unit in changing between G and C.

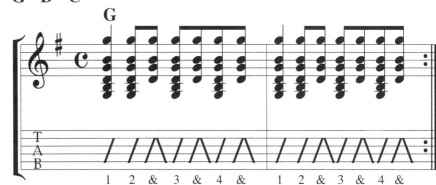

G - C - G - C - G - C - G - C

G - D - C - G - D - C - G - D - C

EXERCISE 23

We'll change the strum we used in Songs 3 - 6 just a little bit by adding one more up stroke on the end.

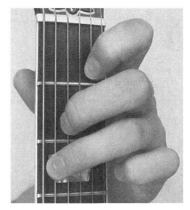

1   2   &   3   &   4   &   1   2   &   3   &   4   &

SONG 8

Now combine these new techniques into the following song, which will be in the key of G . Listen to Song 8 on the CD, **Knocking On Heaven's Door**, to play this. This was a hit for **Bob Dylan** and **Guns N Roses**.

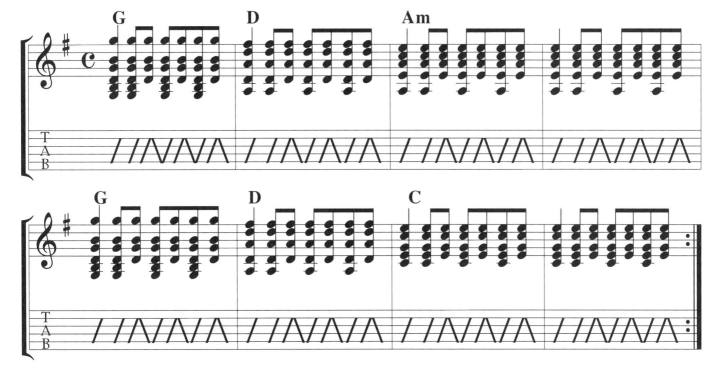

3/4 RHYTHM

Everything we've done so far has been based on 4/4 rhythm or 4 beats per measure. We're going to do an example of 3/4 rhythm which is based on 3 beats per measure. Instead of counting 1 2 3 4, we will be counting 1 2 3, 1 2 3.

This would correspond to a waltz rhythm and there are many common examples.

EXERCISE 24

Practice the following strum:

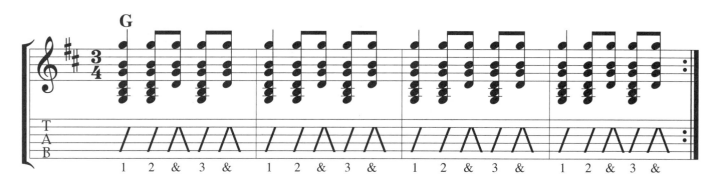

EXERCISE 25

Practice this strum for the D chords. Notice the left hand fingerings.

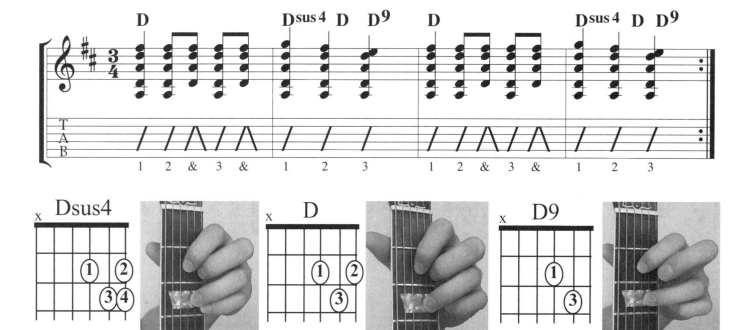

29

SONG 9

We'll use these techniques in a song in 3/4 time. Listen to Song 9 on the CD, **Lucky Man**, to practice this style. This was made popular by **Emerson, Lake, & Palmer**.

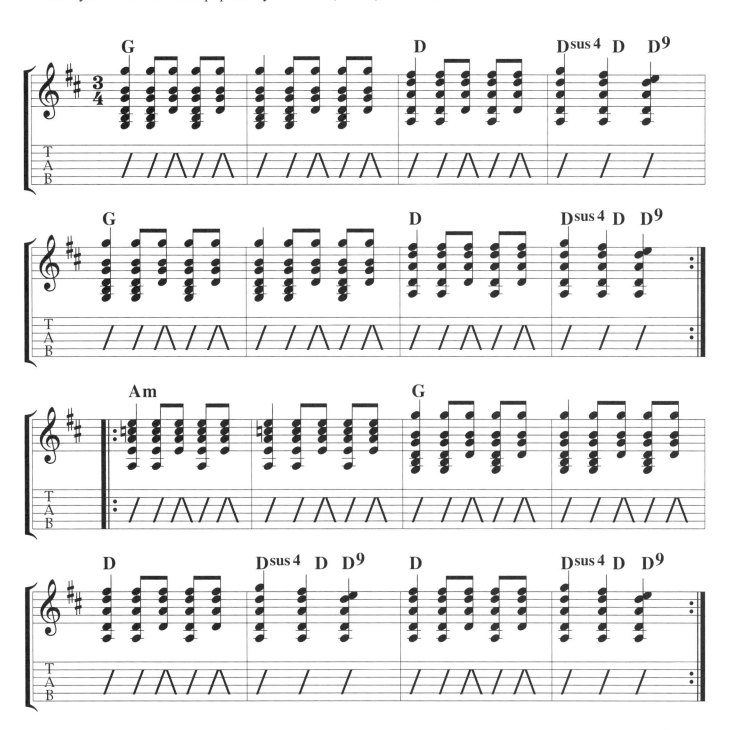

F CHORD

A fairly difficult chord to learn is the F chord. Notice that you have to flatten your index finger so as to fret the first two strings at the 1st fret. Remember the X means don't strum the 5th & 6th strings because they are not in tune with the F chord (F, A, C). Practice the C, F, and G chords.

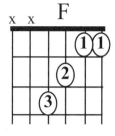

C - F - C - F - C - F - C - F
C - F - G - C - F - G - C - F - G

SONG 10

And now for a song using the F chord in the key of C. Listen to Song 10 on the CD, **Great Balls of Fire**, to play the following example. This was a big hit for **Jerry Lee Lewis**.

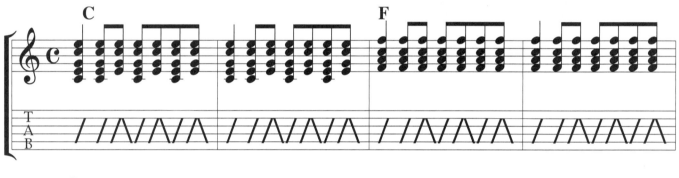

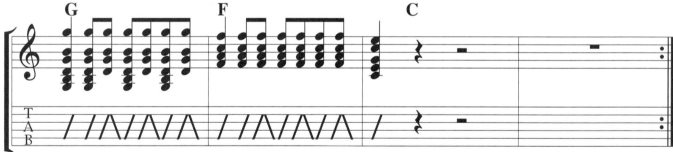

We have covered all of the most common chords that are played in an open position, sometimes called first position. With these chords you will be able to play rhythm to most popular songs. These chords take time to master, so keep practicing and you'll steadily improve.

To study more about chords:

1. Go to the Appendix on page 61 to work on barre chords. Also go to the chord chart on pages 69-71.

2. At this point, you may wish to purchase a songbook at a local music store with songs that you like. You'll be surprised at how many easy songs you can play now that you have mastered this section of the book.

3. You may also consult a guitar teacher who can be of considerable help.

SECTION III
ROCK & ROLL RHYTHM

RIFFS

A very common technique among rock and roll guitar players is the riff. Instead of playing all six strings and strumming as we did in Section II, we will play partial chords and strum two or three strings at a time. We'll start off with two string riffs.

EXERCISE 26

The first riff we'll use is a common rock rhythm and involves playing an A chord riff. The 5th string will be played open and the 4th string will be fretted at the 2nd fret with the left index finger. Pick the 5th and 4th strings only with a very short down stroke (towards the floor). Next place your left ring finger on the 4th string at the 4th fret (this may take some stretching of your left hand) and play a short down stroke hitting only the 5th and 4th strings.

Note that you play two down strokes on each left hand position. We'll play 8 down strokes per measure and will count 1 & 2 & 3 & 4 &. These exercises are shown in tablature with the left hand fingering above the notes in parenthesis. Also note the hand diagrams to make sure you have the correct hand positions.

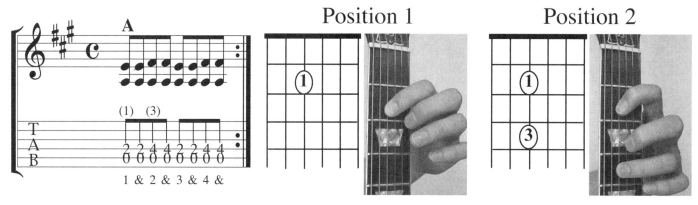

Note that we are using the classical thumb placement, as shown on page 60, on all the riffs in this section.

EXERCISE 27

Using the same fingering but on the 4th and 3rd strings, we'll play a D chord riff.

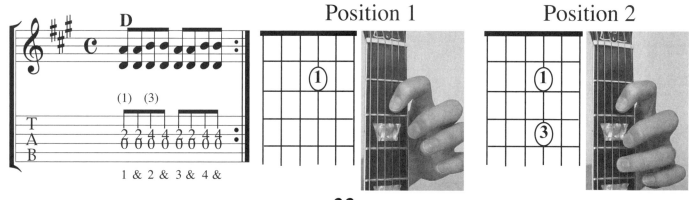

33

EXERCISE 28

The same fingering is used to play the E riff on the 6th and 5th strings.

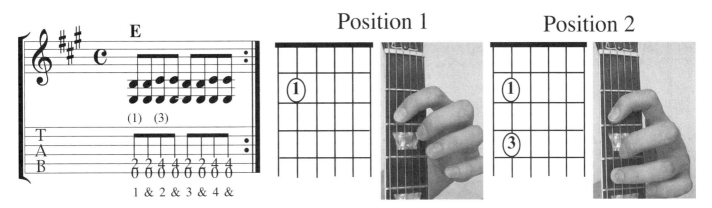

Position 1 ## Position 2

SONG 11

18:22
DVD VIDEO
18-19

We'll combine these three riffs into a very common rock chord progression. This would fit many different songs. Listen to Song 11 on the CD or DVD, **Old Time Rock & Roll**, to play along. This was a big hit for **Bob Seeger.**

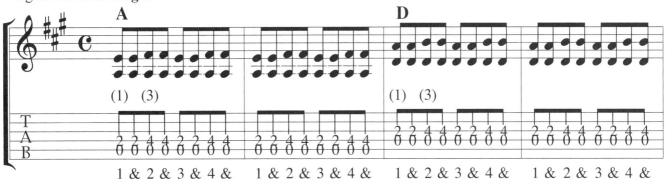

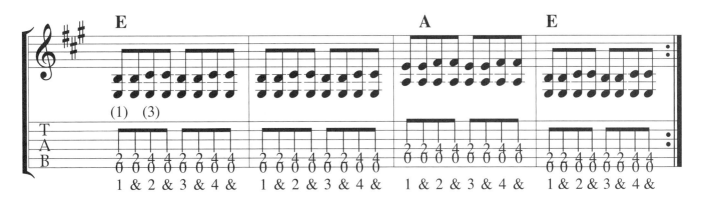

Note - Make sure that you use all down strokes in this song and play and count as smoothly and rhythmically as possible. Try to change between the riffs very smoothly and with no pauses. Play the song slowly at first and when you can change smoothly, speed it up . Listen to the CD or DVD to get the proper timing.

EXERCISE 29

We'll eventually use something else for a B riff, but for now use the following:

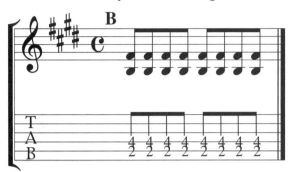 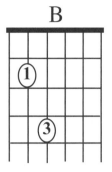 

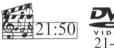

SONG 12

In the same way that we played riffs in the key of A, we can play in the key of E using the E, A, & B riffs. We're going to use a shuffle rhythm with the right hand to play a similar progression. Listen to Song 12 on the CD, **Kansas City**, or **Shuffle In E** on the DVD to get the proper feel for this song. Notice in the DVD, we don't go to the A in the 2nd measure.

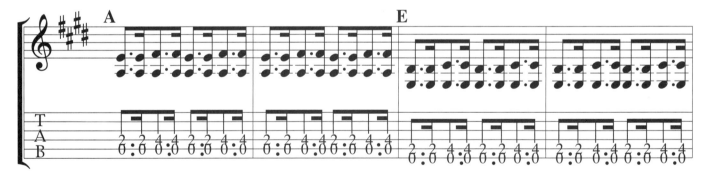

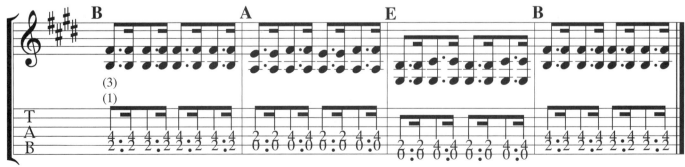

SONG 13

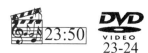

We'll now play a rock shuffle in the key of A. Listen to Song 13 on the CD, **That'll Be The Day**, or **Shuffle In A** on the DVD to play along. This was a big hit for **Buddy Holly** & **Linda Ronstadt**.

POWER CHORDS

26

Exercise 29 is an example of a Power Chord. This is a common technique used to play a heavy percussive rhythm while using only two strings. In Exercise 29 we played a B on the 4th & 5th strings. In the same manner we can play an A chord and a D chord by moving our hand position. Note that the root note is played with the index finger in both examples (the root note is the bass note that corresponds to the chord name, i.e., A is the root note of an A chord).

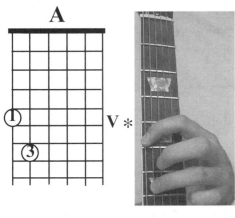

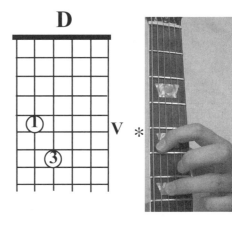

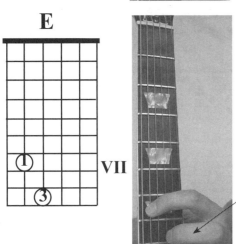

*   The Roman numeral in the chord diagram denotes the fret.

Practice changing between these three power chords:

A - D - E - A - D - E - A - D - E - A - D - E

Note - The middle finger does not press down on the strings in a power chord.

EXERCISE 30   EXERCISE 31

It is very common to play eighth notes with power chords. Practice the following exercises using A & D. Remember to use all down strokes (towards the floor) with your right hand.

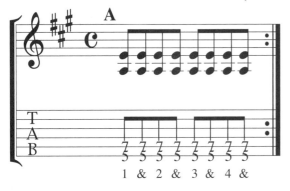

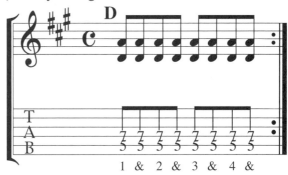

EXERCISE 32

Here's the E power chord.

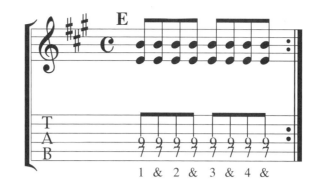

EXERCISE 33

Combine all three power chords into one exercise.

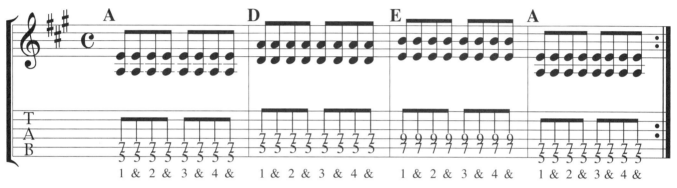

SONG 14

Next we'll use power chords to play another version of **Old Time Rock & Roll**. Play along with Song 14 on the CD or DVD.

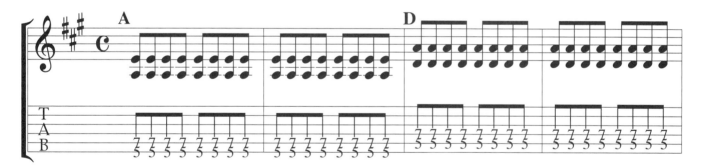

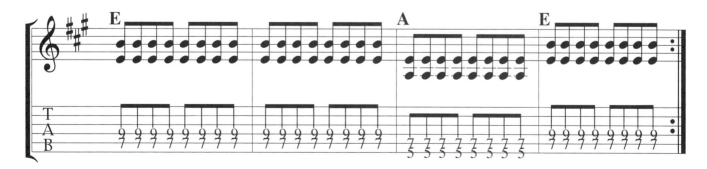

SONG 15

Now we'll use the power chords to play another common chord progression. Play along with Song 15, **12 Bar Blues**, on the CD or DVD.

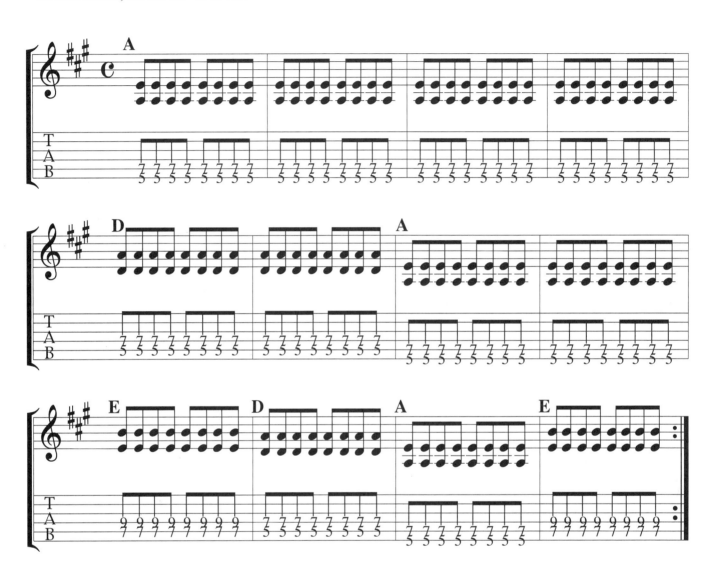

We are playing a couple of the chord progressions with several different techniques. This is to show you that you can use different rhythm styles to play the same song and give it a different feel. If you have more than one guitar player in a band, each player would typically use different techniques to give a bigger sound or layered sound to the music. You can also use more than one technique within the same song. You have to listen closely to the music you are playing and see what sounds the best.

EXERCISE 34

We have been playing in the Key of A starting at the 5th fret. By shifting your hand position down two frets, you can play the G, C, & D chords in the Key of G.

G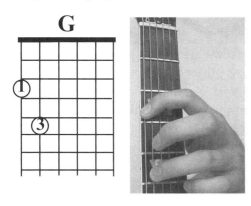

C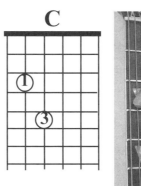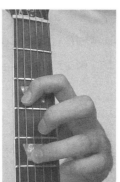

Practice these chord changes:

G - C - D - G - C - D - G - G - C - D - G - C - D - G

SONG 16

We'll use the G, C, and D chords in the following progression. Listen to Song 16, **Rock & Roll Girlfriend,** on the CD or DVD to play along.

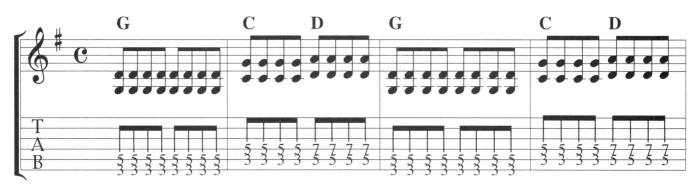

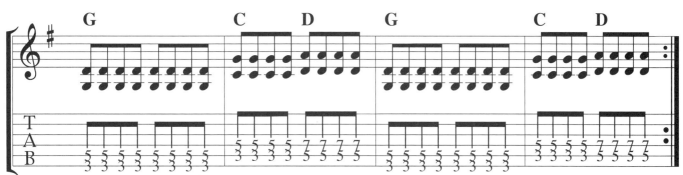

EXERCISE 35

We'll play the Bm power chord at the 7th fret. Practice these chords changes.

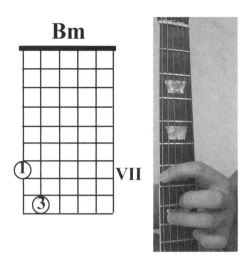

A - Bm - G - A - Bm - G - A - Bm - G

Note - Since we are playing 2 note power chords using the 1st & 5th notes of the scale, these chords could be the major or minor chords. The 3rd note of the scale defines the major or minor. Therefore, the B power chord could be used as a major or minor chord. See the Appendix for more information.

SONG 17

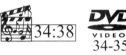

Listen to Song 17 on the CD, **All Along The Watchtower,** or **60's Rock** on the DVD to play the following sequence. Notice that the timing is a little different and also notice the dot over the third note in each measure. This means staccato, i.e. to cut the sound off abruptly. This is done by releasing the pressure on the left hand. Don't lift the fingers off of the strings, simply release the pressure while maintaining contact with the strings. This song was recorded by **Bob Dylan** and **Jimi Hendrix**.

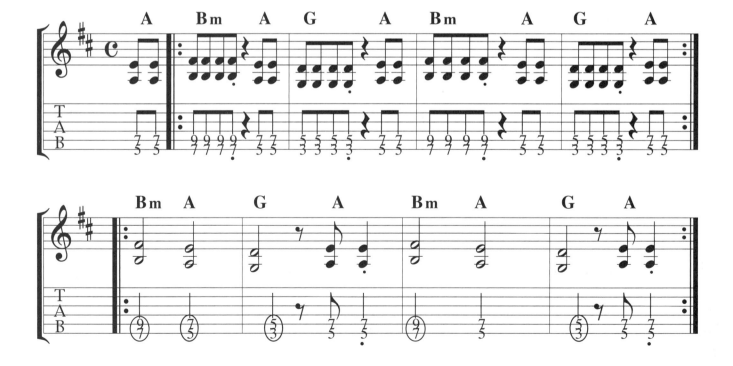

EXERCISE 36

Now we will add an E chord to our repertoire.

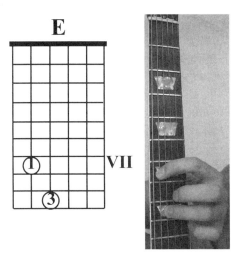

Practice the following chord changes:

E - D - E - D - E - D - E - D - E - D

D - C - D - C - D - C - D - C - D - C

SONG 18

We'll use the E, D, & C power chords in the following progression. Listen to Song 18 on the CD, **Beat It,** to play along. The timing of the right hand will be different on this riff. Listen closely to get it correct. This song was recorded by **Michael Jackson**.

RIGHT HAND DAMPENING

A common technique used by many popular guitarists involves dampening the strings with the heel of the right hand. This is a fairly tricky technique to master, but once you get the hang of it, the dynamics of your guitar playing will improve dramatically.

EXERCISE 37

Lightly place the heel of your right hand on the 6th, 5th, & 4th strings of the guitar next to the bridge. Do not press down firmly, just touch the strings lightly. Check the following diagram, play the exercise, and try to duplicate the sound on the CD.

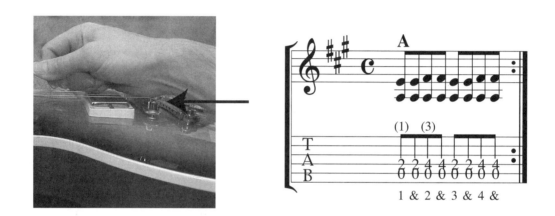

EXERCISE 38

After you have practiced this for a while, go back and play Exercises 26 through 34 and Songs 11 through 16 using this technique. As a general rule, when you are playing eighth notes with riffs or power chords, you would dampen the strings with your right hand.

BARRE CHORD RIFFS

We're going to combine the two styles we have used in this section so far (power chords and riffs). On pages 33-36, we played a rock and roll rhythm using open strings. Now we'll shift up the neck to play the same notes, but in a different position. Again, note that these riffs are based on the bass notes of Barre Chords (the name of the bass note names the chord). Use the right hand dampening technique on all of the barre chord riffs.

This technique will really require some stretching of the left hand. Keep practicing and you'll get the hang of this style. We'll start with the barre chord riffs in the key of A.

EXERCISE 39

Here are the positions for the A Barre Chord Riff:

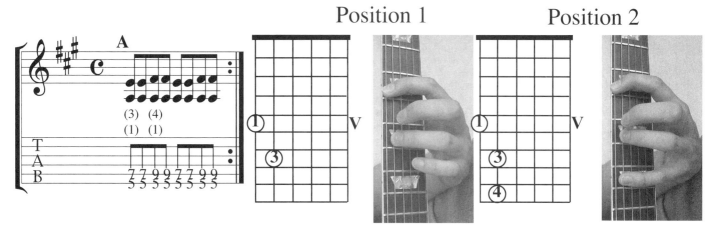

EXERCISE 40

In the same manner we will play the D riff.

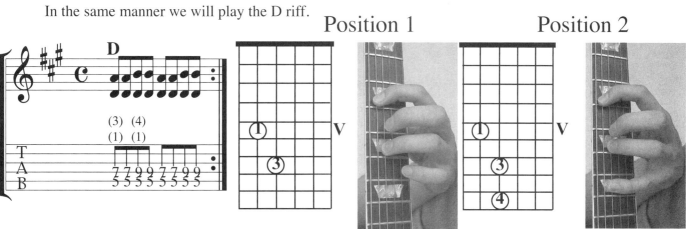

EXERCISE 41

Now the E Riff.

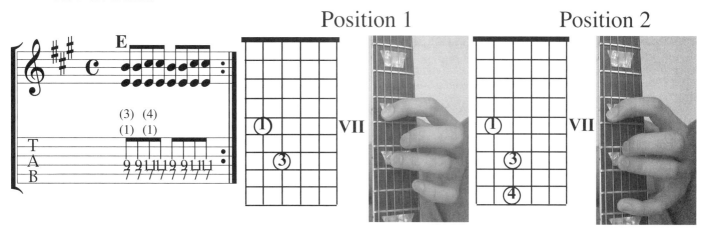

SONG 19

We'll now combine these three barre chord riffs into a common chord progression called the 12 Bar Blues. Listen to Song 19 on the CD to hear another way to play **Johnny B. Goode**. We will use right hand dampening on this song.

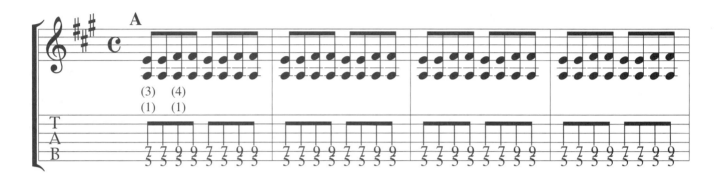

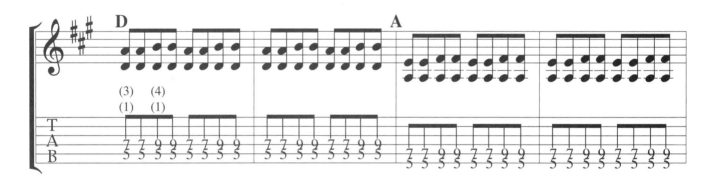

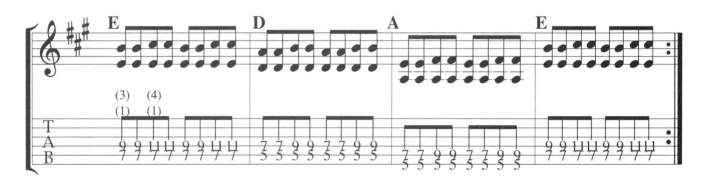

In the same way that you could move the power chords up and down the neck of the guitar, the barre chord riffs can also be moved about the guitar. Since we are not playing any open strings, all of the notes in the chords would be in tune at any position on the guitar neck. To illustrate this we will play something in the key of D using D, G, and A riffs.

EXERCISE 42

We'll use the same finger positions for A and D and we'll add a G chord as follows:

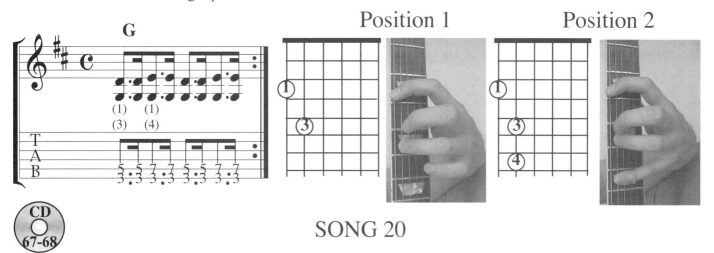

SONG 20

Use these three chords to play the 12 Bar Blues in the key of D. Listen to Song 20 on the CD, **The Wanderer,** to play along with this progression. This was originally made popular by **Dion**. Dampen with the right hand.

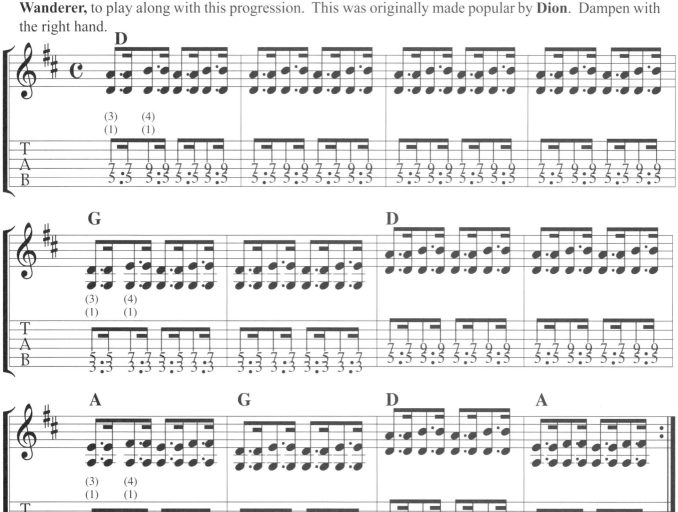

CHORDAL RIFFS

Another style that is very popular uses the 2nd, 3rd, & 4th strings to play a chord. These are based on the Form II Barre chords on page 66. Instead of using the bass strings out of the barre chord, as we did for the riffs and power chords earlier in this section, we're going to use the middle strings out of the chord. We will also deaden the adjacent strings as we did earlier.

EXERCISE 43

Use the left ring finger to hold down the 2nd, 3rd, & 4th strings at the 9th fret to play an E. Touch the 5th string with the tip of your ring finger to deaden it. Also, arch your ring finger in the middle so that the 1st string is not fretted. It should be deadened, too. Strum down on the 4th, 3rd, & 2nd strings. We deaden the strings to help cover up any sloppy right hand technique.

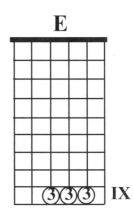

EXERCISE 44

Now use the left index finger to fret the 2nd, 3rd, & 4th strings at the 7th fret to play a D. As we did in Exercise 42, deaden the 5th and 1st strings. Strum down on the 4th, 3rd, & 2nd strings.

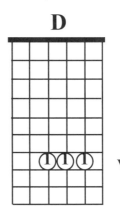

Practice changing between the two chords. You should not move your left hand position, only the index and ring fingers.

E - D - E - D - E - D - E - D

47

SONG 21

Use these same chordal riffs to play along with Song 21 on the CD, **Cocaine**. This was made popular by **Eric Clapton**. Do not use the right hand dampening technique on any of the chordal riffs in this section of the book.

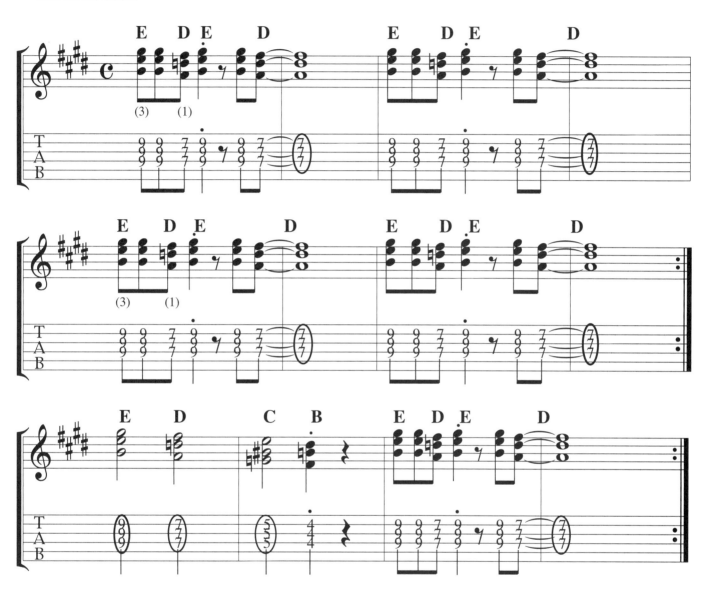

To play the D, C, & B on line 2, use your first finger at the 7th fret for D, the first finger at the 5th fret for C, and the first finger at the 4th fret for B. Make sure you play along with the CD to get the proper timing.

EXERCISE 45

Move down the neck two frets and use the same fingering to play D and C.

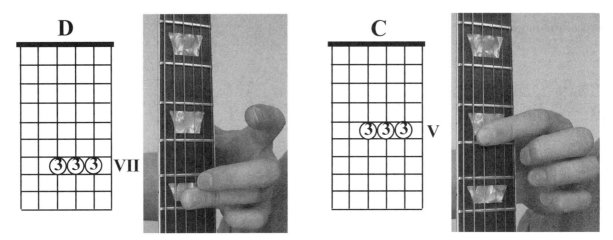

SONG 22

We're going to combine this technique with some single string notes. Note the fingerings. Listen to Song 22 on the CD, **Sunshine Of Your Love,** to play along. This is also an **Eric Clapton** hit.

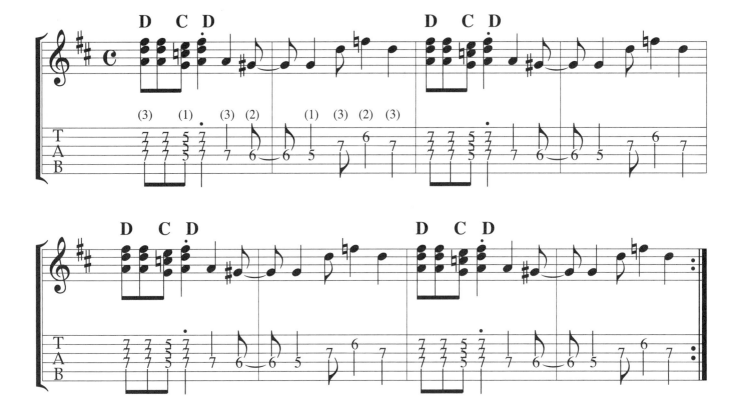

49

EXERCISE 46

A variation on this style adds one voicing note to the chord. Play the D chord as we did in Exercise 45. While still holding down the index finger, use the left middle finger to play the 2nd string at the 8th fret. Strum down to play the Dsus4 chord. Practice changing between the two chords.

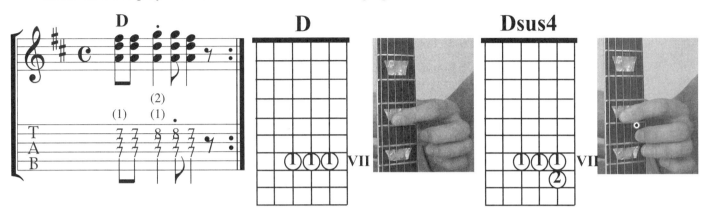

D - Dsus4 - D - Dsus4 - D - Dsus4

EXERCISE 47

Use the same basic finger positions to play the C and Csus4 chords at the 5th fret.

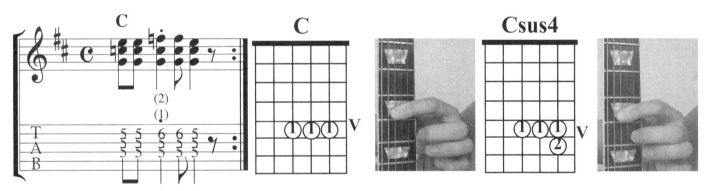

EXERCISE 48

Now play the Bb and Bbsus4 chords at the 3rd fret.

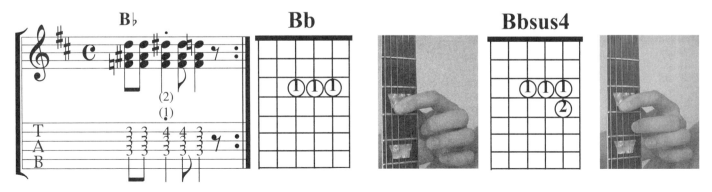

SONG 23

We will use these three chordal riffs to play Song 23 on the CD, **Gimme Shelter,** which was recorded by **The Rolling Stones**. Notice that the timing is a little different. Listen closely to get the exact feel and remember to play all down strokes. We're combining two different styles in this song. The first line is the intro and chorus (chordal riffs) and the second and third lines are the verse (power chords). Dampen with the right hand on the verse.

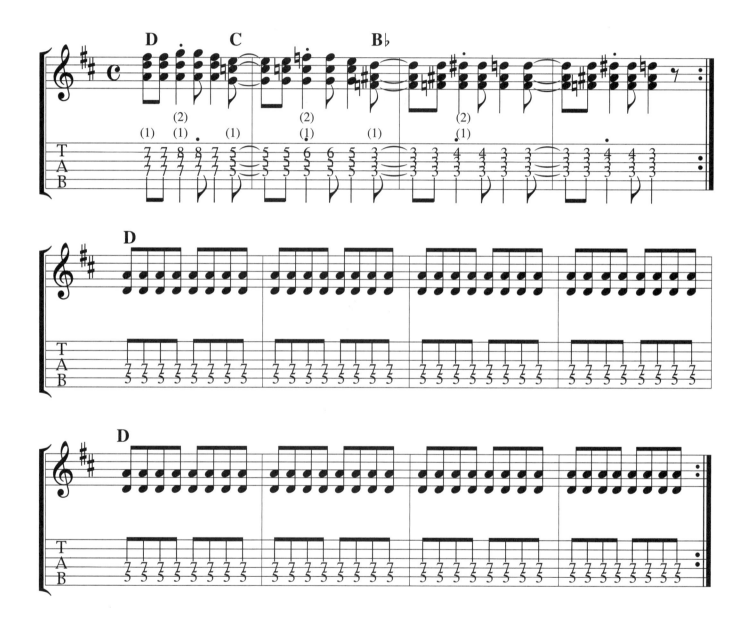

EXERCISE 49

Another variation on this chordal riff would add two notes to the original chord instead of one. We are going to start with a C chord as in Exercise 45. As you play the second string with your middle finger, also put the left ring finger on the 4th string at the 7th fret to play an F chord.

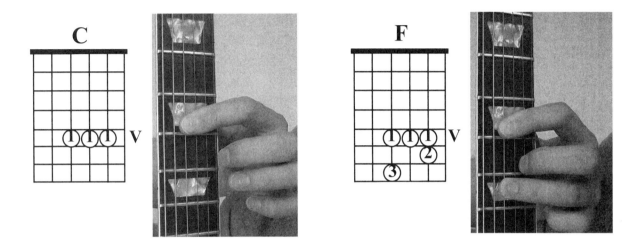

EXERCISE 50

Moving to the 3rd fret, use the same hand positions, and play a Bb chordal riff.

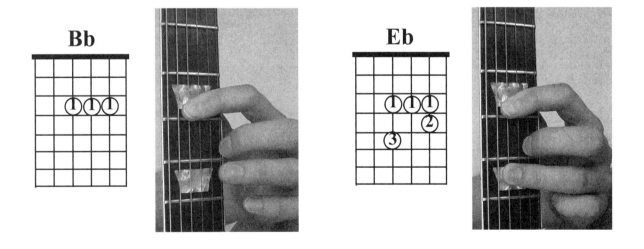

Practice the C chordal riff and the Bb chordal riff until you are comfortable with this finger position. Practice along with the CD.

SONG 24

We will combine three different techniques in the next song. We'll use the C & Bb chordal riffs in line 1, the C & F power chords in line 2, and the C barre chord riff in line 3. Play along with Song 24 on the CD, **Start Me Up**, another hit for **The Rolling Stones**.

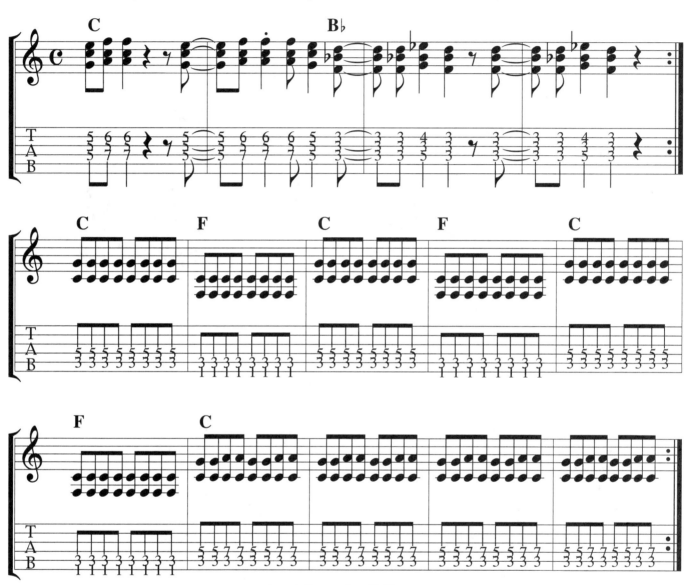

Author's Note

This book is intended to give the beginning electric guitar player a broad understanding of the guitar and the many different styles that can be played. We focused on three different rhythm techniques (as discussed on page 15). You should master all of these techniques. After this you may continue your progress by doing the following:

1. Read pages 62 - 68 in the Appendix and practice the exercises on pages 72.
2. Work through the follow-up courses, *Introduction to Blues Guitar & Introduction to Rock Guitar*, both written by Peter Vogl, to expand your rhythm techniques and learn how to play lead guitar.

SECTION IV
SCALES

EXERCISE 51

Before we play any more scales, we are going to practice an exercise that will help you loosen up your little finger. Most people have difficulty using their pinky until they have developed a little coordination in it. Starting with the 6th string at the 5th fret, play the 5th, 6th, 7th, & 8th frets with the fingers as shown in parenthesis. Continue this up through the 1st string. Use the classical thumb placement as shown on page 60.

When you have become comfortable with this exercise, start with the 1st string @ 8th fret and work back down to the lowest note.

SCALES

In Section I we studied a C scale and applied it to a couple of simple tunes. In this section we are going to work on scales and scale exercises, starting with the G scale in Exercise 52.

EXERCISE 52

Play the **G Scale** using the correct fingering, which is shown in parenthesis above each note. You can use either left thumb placement (page 60).

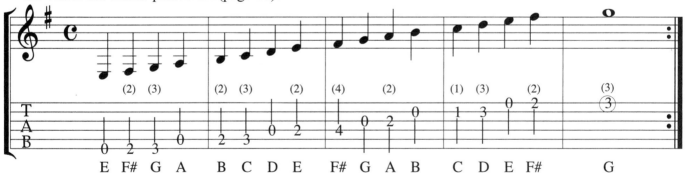

After you have become comfortable with this scale, play it in reverse by starting at the highest note (1st string @ 3rd fret) and working back down the scale.

Scale patterns are the basis of solo playing on the guitar and are included in the next portion of this book for the following reasons:

    1. Scale patterns are easier to play than chords and are useful for developing strength and coordination in your hands and fingers.

    2. You must know scale patterns to be able to improvise (make up your own solos).

SCALE PATTERNS

PATTERN I

We are now going to play scales up the neck of the guitar (no open strings) using basic finger positions. There are five finger patterns for playing a major scale. These can be moved up and down the neck of the guitar to play in any key. We are going to use a G scale as an example of this. The shaded fingerings on the diagram indicate a root note of that scale, which would be a G note in this example. The V indicates the 5th fret.

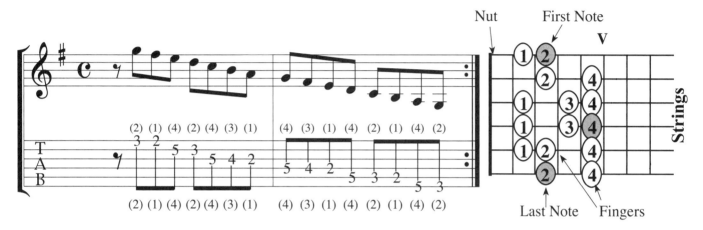

Note - To play an A Scale using Pattern I, move your 2nd finger to the 1st string @ 5th fret and use the same finger pattern. To play other scales, simply place your 2nd finger on the root note on the 1st string and use the same finger pattern.

Pattern II

We'll move up the neck of the guitar to play the G scale using Pattern II. Place your little finger on the 2nd string, 8th fret to get into the proper hand position.

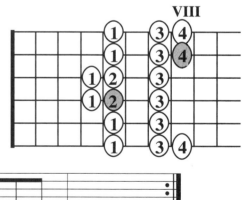

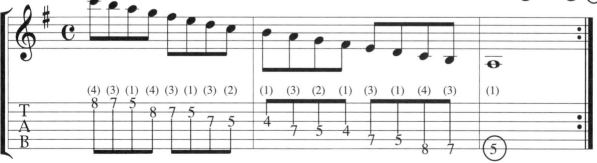

Note - To play an A scale using Pattern II, move your little finger up the neck two frets to find the A note on the 2nd string @ 10th fret. Use this finger pattern to play the A scale. To play other scales using Pattern II, find the root note on the 2nd string and use the same finger pattern at that position.

PATTERN III

Now place your 2nd finger on the 2nd string @ 8th fret and play Pattern III.

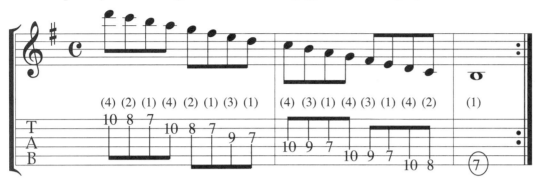

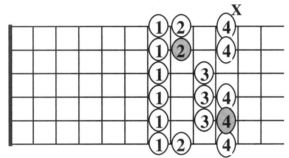

Note - To play other scales using this finger pattern, find the root note on the 2nd string, place your 2nd finger at this position, & use Pattern III to play the scale. Play an E scale by placing your 2nd finger on the 2nd string @ 5th fret & using this pattern.

PATTERN IV

Next find the G note on the 3rd string @ 12th fret, place your 3rd finger there to get into position play Pattern IV.

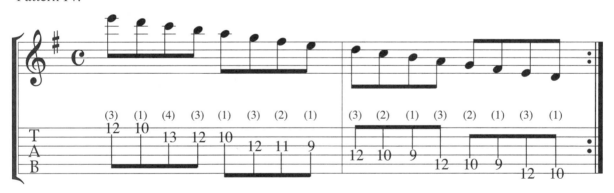

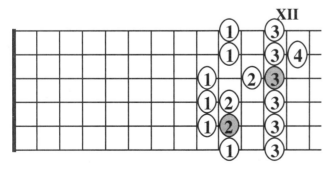

Note - To play other scales using this pattern, find the root note on the 3rd string, place your 3rd finger at this position, & use Pattern IV to play the scale. Try playing a C scale by putting your 3rd finger on the 3rd string @ 5th fret and using this pattern.

57

PATTERN V

Next move your little finger to the 1st string @ 15th fret to play Pattern V.

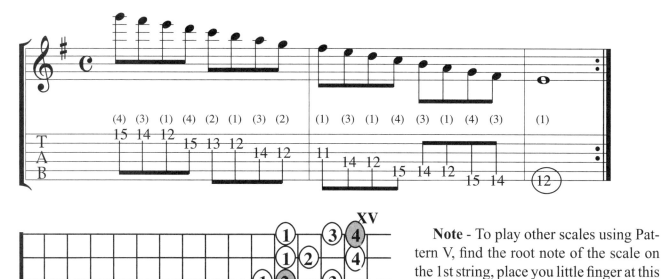

Note - To play other scales using Pattern V, find the root note of the scale on the 1st string, place you little finger at this fret, & use this pattern to play the scale. Play an A scale by placing your little finger on the 1st string @ 5th fret and using this pattern.

The following diagram shows how the patterns overlap on the fret board of the guitar. We are still using a G scale as an example.

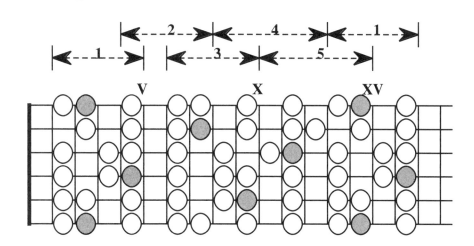

You should practice these scale patterns until you are comfortable with the fingerings in several positions on the guitar neck and you should memorize each finger pattern.

To learn more scales, check out *The Guitarist's Scale Book* which has over 400 scales and modes.

NATURAL MINOR SCALES

Pattern Im

Using the same finger patterns that we used for the major scales, we can play the **natural minor scale**. Use Pattern V in the first position as shown in the following chart. Notice that the natural minor scale uses the b3rd and b7th notes of the scale.

This would correspond to a Form Im7 barre chord at the 3rd fret.

Pattern IIm

Play Pattern I at the second position to play the natural minor scale (IIm). This would correspond to a Dm shape chord at the 6th fret.

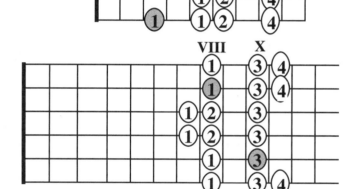

Pattern IIIm

Play Pattern II at the third position to play to play the natural minor scale (IIIm).

Pattern IVm

Play Pattern III at the fourth position to play the natural minor scale (IVm). This would correspond to a Form IIm chord at the 10th fret.

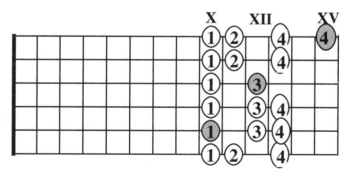

Pattern Vm

Play Pattern V at the fifth position to play the natural minor scale (Vm).

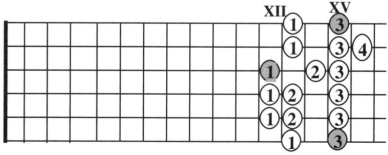

LEFT HAND POSITION

When playing, the position of the left thumb on the back of the neck is very important because it is used to brace and balance the left hand. There are two common thumb placements shown below and we'll use each of them, depending on the techniques we're playing.

A. Classical Thumb Placement

This thumb position is used by all classical guitarists. In this position the middle of the thumb contacts the middle of the guitar neck. See the following diagrams:

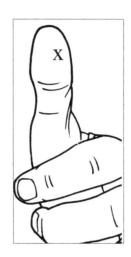
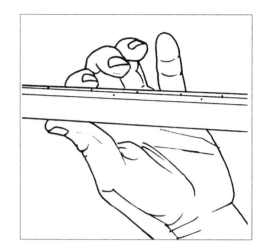

B. Elevated Thumb Placement

This position is used by the vast majority of popular guitarists. In this position the first joint of the thumb makes contact with the middle of the guitar neck. Check the following diagrams:

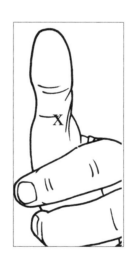
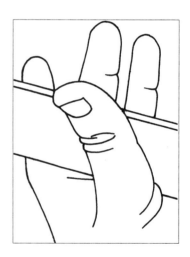

A CHORD

If you are still having trouble with the A chord after practicing the fingering on page 17 for a few weeks, try these alternate fingerings:

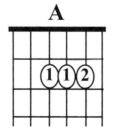
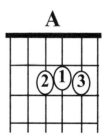

G CHORD

If you still cannot form the G chord after practicing the fingering on page 26 for several weeks, try this fingering:

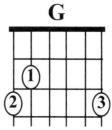

APPENDIX

MUSIC THEORY

We have been referring to this section throughout the book, so hopefully you have been studying it all along. To become an accomplished guitarist you must understand some basic principals about the guitar and music in general so that you can get the overall picture of the music you are playing.

In Sections I & IV we studied scales. A major scale consists of 7 notes, which we will number 1-7.

Notes In Major Scales

Scale		1	2	3	4	5	6	7
Key of C		C	D	E	F	G	A	B
Key of G	(1#)	G	A	B	C	D	E	F#
Key of D	(2#)	D	E	F#	G	A	B	C#
Key of A	(3#)	A	B	C#	D	E	F#	G#
Key of E	(4#)	E	F#	G#	A	B	C#	D#
Key of F	(1b)	F	G	A	Bb	C	D	E
Key of Bb	(2b)	Bb	C	D	Eb	F	G	A
Key of Eb	(3b)	Eb	F	G	Ab	Bb	C	D
Key of Ab	(4b)	Ab	Bb	C	Db	Eb	F	G

A **chromatic scale** consists of 12 notes, all the notes possible to play in one octave. All of the notes are shown below. The notes on top of each other are identical. For instance, the A# and the Bb are the same. These are called **Enharmonic Tones**.

Chromatic Scale

1	2	3	4	5	6	7	8	9	10	11	12
A	A#	B	C	C#	D	D#	E	F	F#	G	G#
	Bb			Db		Eb			Gb		Ab

Notice that there is no note between B & C, and no note between E & F. A **half step** is one note in the chromatic scale (A to A# is a half step). This corresponds to one fret on the guitar. A **whole step** is two notes in the chromatic scale (A to B is a whole step). This corresponds to two frets on the guitar.

To figure out the notes in any major scale, use the following guides:

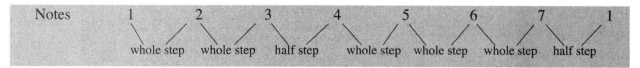

For example, to figure out the notes in an A Scale, start with an A note in the chromatic scale. To go to note 2, make a whole step to B (2 frets on the guitar). Note 3 would be a whole step to C#. Note 4 is a half step to D (1 fret on the guitar). Note 5 is a whole step to E. Note 6 is a whole step to F#. Note 7 is a whole step to G#. Note 1 is a half step back to A.

In Sections II & III we studied chords and partial chords or riffs. A relationship exists between scales and chords known as **chord progressions**. We started with several three chord songs. The most common chords used are the 1st, 4th, & 5th chords of a key. For example, we first played in the key of A, using the A, D, & E chords. There are many songs that use only these three chords.

The following chart shows the common chord progressions that you will encounter:

Common Chords		Commonly Called	Example
1st	1st note of scale (major chord)	(Tonic) A	
4th	4th note of scale (major chord)	(Subdominant)	D
5th	5th note of scale (major chord)	(Dominant)	E
6th minor	6th note of scale (minor chord)	(Relative Minor)	F#m
2nd	2nd note of scale (major chord)		B
2nd minor	2nd note of scale (minor chord)		Bm
3rd	3rd note of scale (major chord)		C#
3rd minor	3rd note of scale (minor chord)		C#m
b7th	7th note of scale moved down a half step (major chord)		G
1 (7th)	1st note of scale (dominant 7th chord) $1 \rightarrow 1 (7th) \rightarrow 4$		A7
5 (7th)	5th note of scale (dominant 7th chord) $5 \rightarrow 5 (7th) \rightarrow 1$		E7
b3rd	3rd note of scale moved down a half step (major chord)		C
b6th	6th note of scale moved down a half step (major chord)		F

A **major chord** consists of three notes, the 1st, 3rd, & 5th notes of that particular scale. Although we are often strumming 6 strings at a time, we are only playing a combination of three notes. For example, the first chord we played was an A chord, which consists of A, C#, & E. The 6 notes played when you strum an open A chord are E, A, E, A, C#, & E.

A **minor chord** consists of three notes, the 1st, b3rd, & 5th notes of that scale. The minor sound comes from lowering the 3rd a half step. An Am chord is composed of A, C, & E.

A **dominant 7th chord**, commonly called the 7th chord, is a four note chord consisting of the 1st, 3rd, 5th, & b7th notes of that scale. The 7th sound comes from adding the b7th note (7th lowered a half step). For example, an A7 chord is composed of A, C#, E, & G.

A **minor 7th chord** consists of the 1st, b3rd, 5th, & b7th notes of that scale. For example, an Am7 is composed of A, C, E, & G.

The following chart shows what notes these and other common chords are composed of:

Chord	Notes	Example	
Major	1st, 3rd, 5th	A	A, C#, E
7th	1st, 3rd, 5th, b7th	A7	A, C#, E, G
Minor	1st, b3rd, 5th	Am	A, C, E
Minor 7th	1st, b3rd, 5th, b7th	Am7	A, C, E, G
Major 7th	1st, 3rd, 5th, 7th	Amaj7	A, C#, E, G#
9th	1st, 2nd, 3rd, 5th, b7th	A9	A, B, C#, E, G
sus4	1st, 3rd, 4th, 5th	Asus4	A, C#, D, E
Diminished	1st, b3rd, b5th, 6th	Adim	A, C, Eb, F
Augmented	1st, 3rd, #5th	A+	A, C#, F

63

CIRCLE OF 5THS

The circle of 5ths is useful for memorizing the order of sharps or flat keys, as well as the order in which the sharps or flats occur.

Beginning with the key of C and moving clockwise in steps of 5ths, each key has one more sharp than the one before it. Moving counterclockwise from C in steps of 4ths, each key has one more flat than the one before it.

Each new sharp is the 7th of the key in which it occurs. Each new flat is the 4th of the key in which it occurs.

The key signatures as they would appear in music notation are shown inside the circle. To figure out the name of the flat keys from the key signature, use the next to last flat. Move the last sharp up one note (1/2 step or 1 fret) to figure out the name of the sharp keys.

Notice that there are 12 different major keys, but three of them have different names. Keys that have the same key signature, but have different names are called Enharmonic keys.

The relative minor key of each major key, which is the 6th of that key, is shown inside the circle. The relative minor has the same key signature as its relative major key.

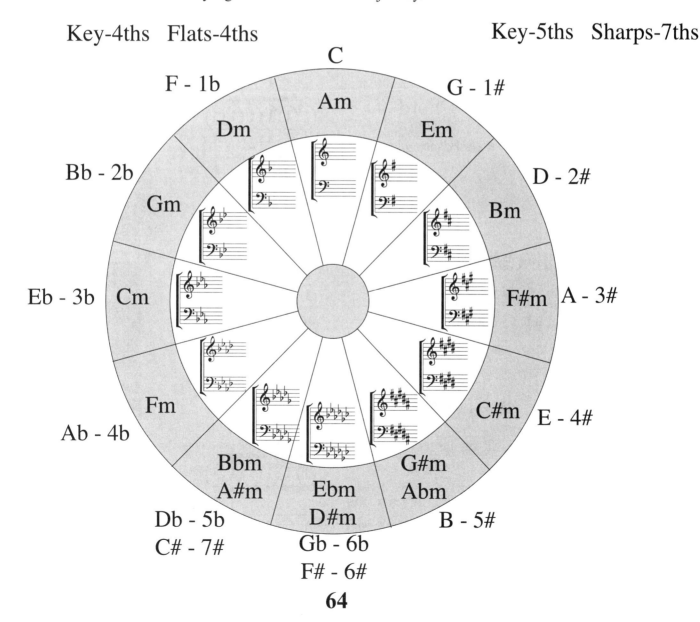

64

BARRE CHORDS

A fairly common but difficult technique to learn is the barre chord. Using the classical thumb placement, place your left index finger at the first fret. Stretch the finger across all 6 strings and press down very firmly. All 6 strings should ring out very clearly when you strum down.

Form I Major Chord

F

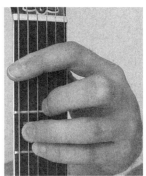

The first chord we'll play using the barre is an F chord. You'll notice from the diagram that this is similar to playing an E chord along with the barre. This is sometimes called an E Shape Barre Chord, but we are going to refer to it as a Form I Barre Chord. Note that the root note (F) is on the 6th string.

This will take some practice, but don't get discouraged. Try forming this chord for a short while each practice session and you'll soon be getting the hang of it.

Form I Dominant 7th Chord

F7

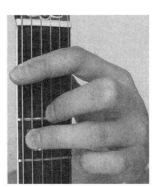

Lift your little finger off of the strings to form the F7 chord.

Form I Minor Chord

Fm

Go back to the F chord and lift your 2nd finger off the frets to form the Fm chord.

Form I Minor 7th Chord

Lift your little finger off of the strings to play the Fm7 chord.

Fm7

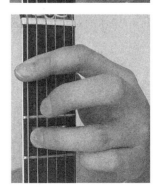

Note that by keeping the barre at the first fret and simply moving your fingers around, you can play four different chords with this same basic hand position.

Form II Major Chord

By taking the basic position for the open A chord, we can barre at the 1st fret and play a Bb chord, which we will call a Form II Barre Chord. This is also called an A shaped Barre Chord. Note that you have to cover the 2nd, 3rd, & 4th strings with the ring finger. Also note that the root note (Bb) is on the 5th string.

Bb

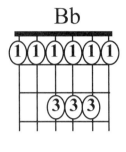

If you have trouble with this chord because of small fingers, try this alternate fingering:

Bb

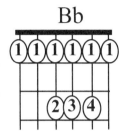

Form II Dominant 7th Chord

Shift your fingers to the following position to play the Bb7 chord.

Bb7

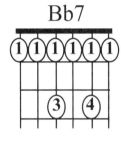

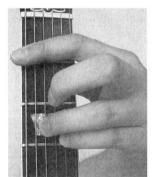

Form II Minor Chord

To play the Bb minor chord, you will have to shift your fingers around to the following position.

Bbm

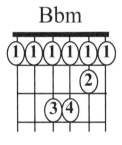

Form II Minor 7th Chord

Lift your little finger off of the strings to play the Bbm7 chord.

Bbm7

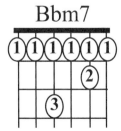

These chords are the basis for the Power Chords we played in Section III. We used the 5th & 6th strings of the Form I chord and the 5th & 4th strings of the Form II chord. The Form II chord is also the basis for the chordal riffs that we played. We used the 2nd, 3rd, & 4th strings of the major chord.

Form III Major Chord

Another type of barre chord that isn't as common as the first two is the C shape barre chord. Again, barre at the first fret and arrange your fingers in the following position to play the Db chord. Note that the root note (Db) is on the 5th string.

This chord is the basis for the 2nd position chordal riff we used on Songs 23 - 24. Again we used the 2nd, 3rd, & 4th strings.

Db

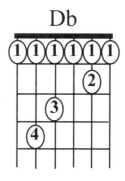

Form III Dominant 7th Chord

This chord is the same as moving the C7 chord up the neck. Be sure to deaden the 1st and 6th strings.

The Form III minor and minor 7th chords are not commonly played out of a barre chord position.

Db7

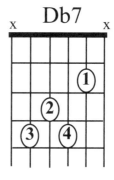

These chords can be moved around the neck of the guitar, since we are playing no open strings. The following chart shows what chord you are actually playing when you form the chords at different frets. The fret numbers refer to the position you form the barre.

Fret	Form I	Form II	Form III
1	F	A# or Bb	C# or Db
2	F# or Gb	B	D
3	G	C	D# or Eb
4	G# or Ab	C# or Db	E
5	A	D	F
6	A# or Bb	D# or Eb	F# or Gb
7	B	E	G
8	C	F	G# or Ab
9	C# or Db	F# or Gb	A
10	D	G	A# or Bb
11	D# or Eb	G# or Ab	B
12	E	A	C
13	F	A# or Bb	C# or Db

You should practice these chords for a few minutes each practice session. Don't spend all of your practice time on them, just 5 minutes or so each session, and in a few weeks you'll be getting the hang of them.

FINDING COMMON CHORDS

The following charts show how to find the proper chord position for all of the common chords in a key when using barre chords. The first chart shows how to find the chords if the 1 chord is a Form I Chord. The second chart shows how to find the common chords when the 1 Chord is a Form II chord. The move column shows the fret position relative to the 1 chord.

Chord	Example	Common Position			Optional Position		
		Barre Type	Position	Move	Barre Type	Position	Move
1	A	Form I	@ 5th fret				
2m	Bm	Form IIm	@ 2nd fret	Down 3 frets	Form Im	@ 7th fret	Up two frets
3m	C#m	Form IIm	@ 4th fret	Down 1 fret	Form Im	@ 9th fret	Up 4 frets
4	D	Form II	@ 5th fret	Same fret	Form I	@ 10th fret	Up 5 frets
5	E	Form II	@ 7th fret	Up two frets	Form I	@ 12th fret	Up 7 frets
6m	F#m	Form Im	@ 2nd fret	Down 3 frets	Form IIm	@ 9th fret	Up 4 frets
b7	G	Form I	@ 3rd fret	Down 2 frets	Form II	@ 10th fret	Up 5 frets

Chord	Example	Common Position			Optional Position		
		Barre Type	Position	Move	Barre Type	Position	Move
1	D	Form II	@ 5th fret				
2m	Em	Form Im	Open	Down 5 frets	Form IIm	@ 7th fret	Up 2 frets
3m	F#m	Form Im	@ 2nd fret	Down 3 frets	Form IIm	@ 9th fret	Up 4 frets
4	G	Form I	@ 3rd fret	Down 2 frets	Form II	@ 10th fret	Up 5 frets
5	A	Form I	@ 5th fret	Same fret	Form II	@ 12th fret	Up 7 frets
6m	Bm	Form Im	@ 7th fret	Up 2 frets	Form IIm	@ 2nd fret	Down 3 frets
b7	C	Form I	@ 8th fret	Up 3 frets	Form II	@ 3rd fret	Down 2 frets

CHORD CHART

There is a chord chart on the following three pages that shows all of the common chords you will encounter. Notice that they are laid out in sequence with all of the different type chords on the same line. For instance, all of the different A chords are on the second line. They are also aligned vertically in finger patterns. For example, all of the Form I Barre Chords are in the second column on the first page.

The small x on top of the chord diagram means don't strum this string because it would be a note that is not in the chord. The Roman numeral at the right side of the chord shows the fret position of the index finger.

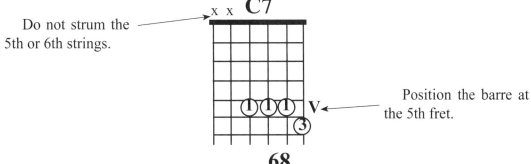

Do not strum the 5th or 6th strings.

Position the barre at the 5th fret.

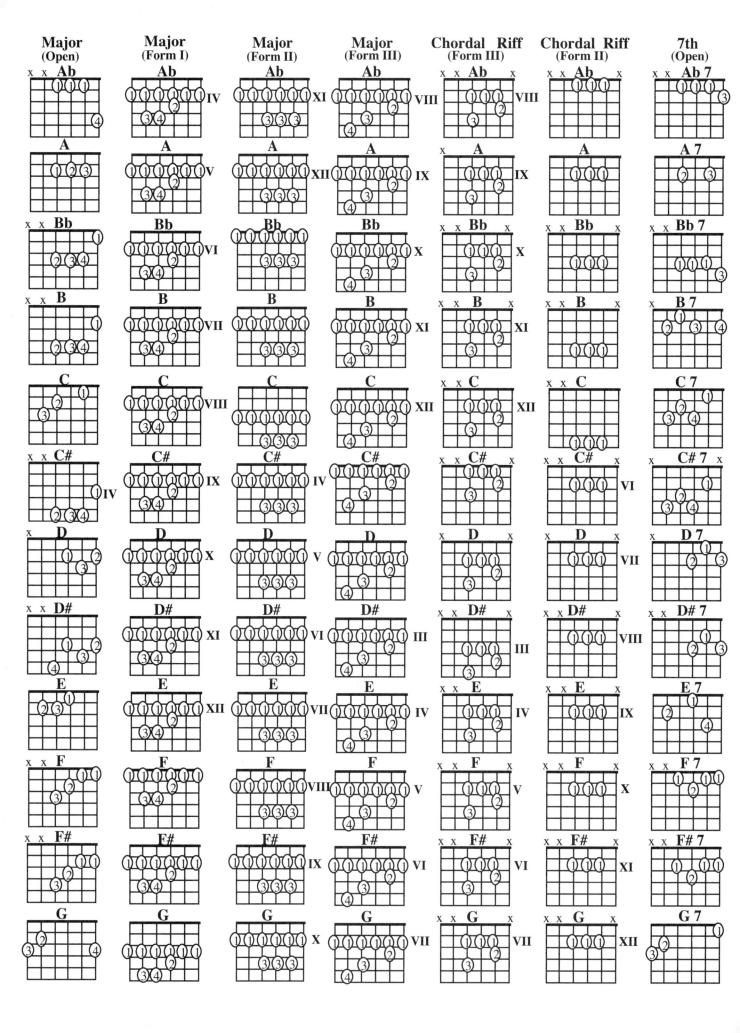

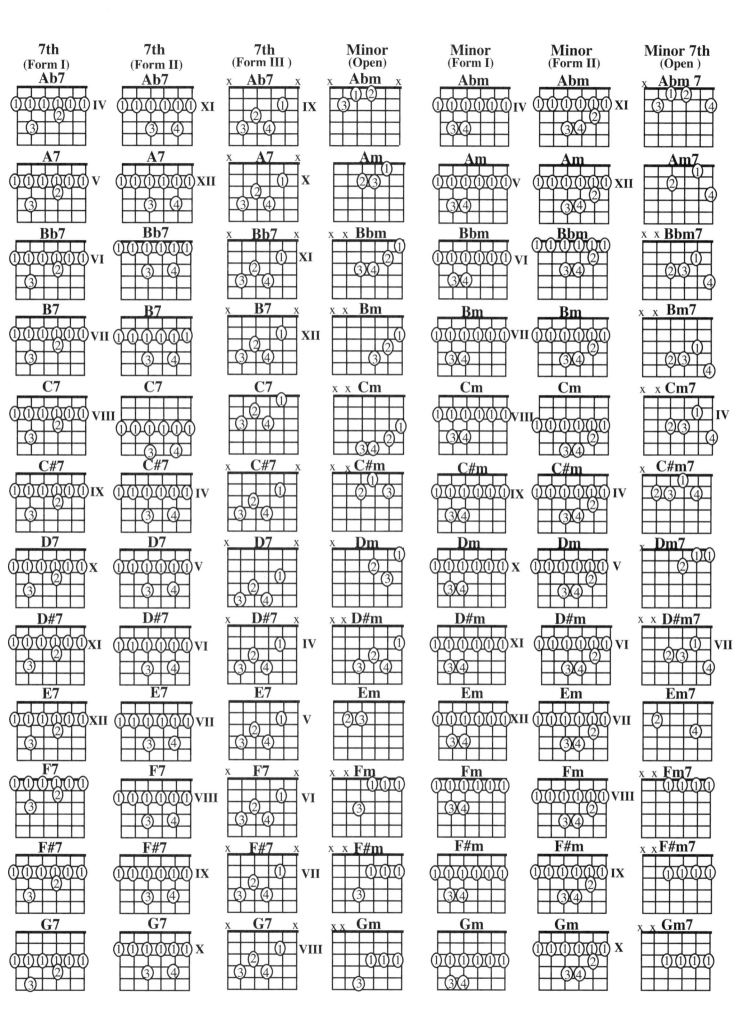

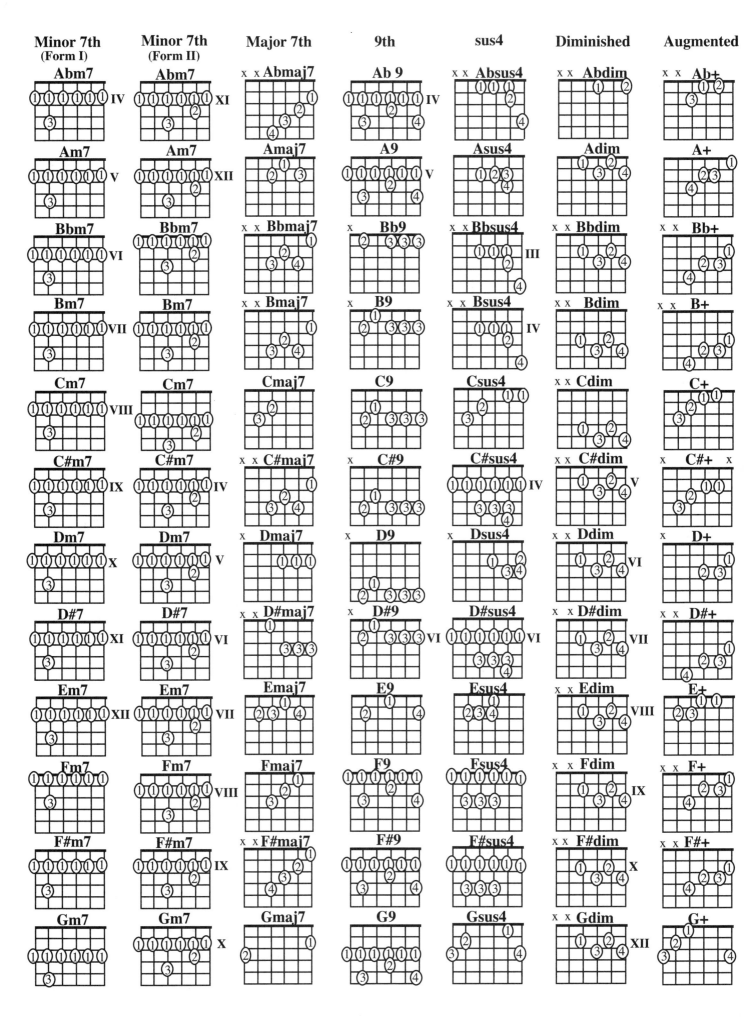

SUBSTITUTING BARRE CHORDS

Using the chords on the preceding pages will make your playing much fuller and more interesting. Play the following exercises to practice these chords.

EXERCISE 56

We will use the following barre chords to play **Johnny B. Goode** on page 23.

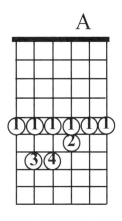
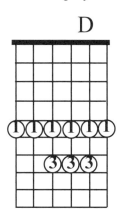
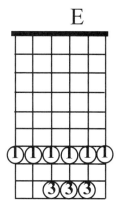

EXERCISE 57

Using the same barre chords for A, D, & E, play Songs 1 & 2 on page 20 and Song 4.

EXERCISE 58

Using the following barre chords for Em, Am, & B7, play Songs 5 & 6 on pages 24 & 25.

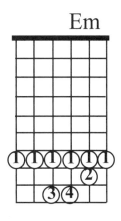
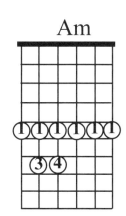
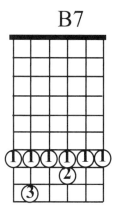

EXERCISE 59

Substitute barre chords for the other songs in Section II. Use the chord chart and the charts on page 68 as guides. Play along with the CD to practice the barre chords.

For more chords, try *The Guitarist's Chord Book* which has over 900 chords with diagrams & photos.

What To Do Next

Taking private lessons from a qualified teacher is always a good idea. Check with your local music store to find a good instructor.

Blues Guitar Deluxe Edition by Peter Vogl is a followup to the Electric Guitar course that teaches more advanced rhythm to the 12 Bar Blues and soloing using the minor pentatonic and blues scales. It covers many popular techniques that blues players use and also contains a hot licks section.

Book/DVD/CD $15.95

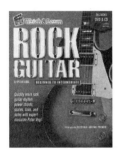

Rock Guitar Deluxe Edition by Peter Vogl is another followup course that teaches more advanced rhythm techniques and lead playing using the minor pentatonic scales. It shows all the techniques that legendary rock guitarists use to get those famous sounds. It also contains a hot licks section.

Book/DVD/CD $15.95

To find these courses, contact your local music store or try the number and address on the back cover of this book. You can also look up our web site at **cvls.com**.

Video & Audio Downloads Available
download@cvls.com